The Force of Reason

The Force of Reason

An Introduction to Habermas'
Theory of Communicative Action

Arie Brand

ALLEN & UNWIN
Sydney Wellington London Boston

© Arie Brand 1990

First published in 1990
Allen & Unwin Australia Pty Ltd
An Unwin Hyman company
8 Napier Street, North Sydney, NSW 2059 Australia

Allen & Unwin New Zealand Limited
75 Ghuznee Street, Wellington, New Zealand

Unwin Hyman Limited
15–17 Broadwick Street, London W1V 1FP, England

Allen & Unwin Inc.
8 Winchester Place, Winchester, Mass 01890 USA

National Library of Australia
Cataloguing-in-Publication entry:

Brand, Arie, 1936–
    The force of reason: an introduction to Habermas'
    Theory of communicative action.

    Bibliography.
    Includes index.
    ISBN 0 04 442157 5
    ISBN 0 04 370190 6 (pbk)

    1. Habermas, Jurgen, 1929–   . Theorie des
    Kommunikativen Handelns. 2. Sociology –
    Philosophy. 3. Communcation – Philosophy.
    4. Social action. 5. Functionalism (Social sciences).
    6. Rationalism. I. Title.

301′.01

Library of Congress Catalog Card Number: 89-0848

Typeset by Times Graphics, Singapore
Printed by SRM Production Services Sdn Bhd,
Malaysia

Contents

Preface

The book entitled *The Theory of Communicative Action* has a special place in Habermas' work, because of its extraordinary size and, even more so, its remarkable scope. There is in sociological literature nothing quite like it, with the possible exception of Parsons' *The Structure of Social Action*, which dates now from more than half a century ago. In both works we find an attempt, not just to provide one more review of classical theory, but to reshape the whole intellectual terrain in such a fashion that it accommodates the views of the reviewer.

The importance of the *Theory of Communicative Action* is, however, matched by its inaccessibility. Presentation was never Habermas' strongest side. 'The reader', says a German reviewer, who is a considerable theorist in his own right, 'has to climb steep heights, hurry through wide plains, go over dangerously narrow ridges and winding paths. From time to time there are menacing masses of theory on the side in front of which one cannot tarry, intimidated, because one has hardly looked around or the author presses further forward' (Bubner, 1982: 342–43). The professional teacher might, for a while, enjoy the sensation of being an intellectual mountain guide, until he or she has the alarming experience of having lost the group.

This book is written for the advanced student who wants some preparation before undertaking the study of Habermas' main work. It is also written for those who have to assist students in this arduous undertaking. These didactic aims have been predominant. Therefore the presentation of Habermas' views has been strictly separated from critical comments on them. No attempt has been made here to discuss other works of Habermas, unless this was necessary to gain a better understanding of *The Theory of Communicative Action*. The difficult question of to what extent this latter work fits in with his earlier views, particularly those unfolded in *Knowledge and Human Interests*, has been entirely left aside here.

Habermas presents his own views on communicative action simultaneously with his comments on the classical theorists. For the sake of clarity of presentation these two elements have been separated in this introductory book. Thus, in the first part of this book an attempt is made to trace the main outlines of Habermas' theory. The intellectual map so acquired is then given detail in the second part by looking at his comments on his predecessors. The last chapter offers, finally, an overview of the main points of criticism.

Introduction

Habermas' work is informed by the basic conviction that history is the arena for the operation of reason. This would seem to place him in the tradition of German historical idealism, that brand of the philosophy of history which, as Hegel said, only had one thought to bring with it: 'the simple thought of reason, that reason rules the world'.

Habermas might go along with this statement in its sweeping generality. Where he becomes specific on this point, he immediately parts company with Hegel. To Habermas reason operates in history not (as Hegel has it) because human beings are more or less passive puppets in the grand movements of some Absolute Spirit, but because they themselves have, as a species, a capacity for rationality. Reason is, for him, a human disposition for rationality which is inherent in the use of speech. Language is the vehicle for the most basic form of social action, namely communicative action.

Though the capacity for rationality is a competence of the human species as such, the possibilities for it do not appear, ready-made and complete, on the historical scene. There is a process of social evolution here, in which social integration, for Habermas (who follows Durkheim here) originally a matter of the ritual use of sacred symbols, becomes more and more a matter of communicative action through language. The scope for communicative rationality widens over time with the unfolding of the linguistic possibilities for reason. Habermas uses the term rationalisation to indicate this process. He suggests that there is in language itself a thrust to the achievement of a general situation in which shared understanding is rationally motivated rather than based on a tradition to which people are more or less passively subject.

We might well ask, at this point, whether Habermas pictures

social evolution as the development of society being made more and more safe for communicative rationality, as it were, or whether he has just found more impressive terms to dress up an eighteenth- and nineteenth-century belief in progress. This would put him in the illustrious, though by now somewhat suspect, company of those Enlightenment philosophers who regarded intellectual progress as a condition for moral progress. In a way this is exactly what Habermas does. The collective learning process which advances communicative rationality can also lead to ethical progress. The most tangible expression of this is found in the field of law.

Here is where Habermas is a revolutionary, while at the same time placing himself in an older tradition of European social thought. He is a revolutionary in daring to talk of 'ethical progress'—without using this actual term—in an era in which this notion has been all but discredited. In doing so he links his thought (though, as we will see, in a very qualified fashion) not only to that of the Enlightenment but also to that of those founding fathers of sociology who took the existence of ethical progress for granted. De Tocqueville was still ambiguous on this point because, rather than stressing the desirability of the social evolution he perceived, he emphasised its inevitability. For him social evolution consisted of the movement towards equality which was universal and durable and eluded all human interference. For Spencer, however, the 'ultimate development of the ideal man' was 'logically certain'. For Comte the fundamental type of human evolution consisted of 'the increasing ascendancy of our humanity over our animal nature, in accordance with the double supremacy of intelligence over our inclinations, and the sympathetic over the personal instinct' (quoted in Ginsberg, 1961:3,17).

With Weber, who regarded rationalisation as the steady progression towards meaninglessness and the loss of freedom, this optimistic temper had already clearly disappeared. This was also the case with Habermas' immediate predecessors in the Frankfurt School whose—on this point—Weberian ideas were reinforced by close personal involvement in the history of some of the most gruesome decades of this century. Habermas is of a different opinion, no doubt for a variety of reasons; those which can be identified have to do in the first place with his personal life experience and second with his general philosophical outlook.

On the first point we should keep in mind that Habermas is more than a generation younger than such representatives of the Frankfurt School as Horkheimer and Adorno and that while the latter were already middle-aged at the end of the war Habermas was then only an adolescent. He states about his postwar experiences: 'I am ... ambivalent because I have the impression that something is deeply amiss in the rational society in which I grew up and in which I now live. On the other hand, I have also retained something else from the experience of 1945 and after, namely that things got better. Things really got rather better. One must use that as a starting point too' (Dews, 1986:74, 126).

On the second point, that of the difference in general philosophical outlook, Habermas has claimed that the deep pessimism about the rationalisation process, which his immediate predecessors in the Frankfurt School shared with Weber, was also a matter of their imprisonment within the wrong philosophical paradigm, that of what Habermas calls the philosophy of consciousness. This allegedly caused them to have a far too restrictive view of rationality, in which this was identified with only one of its aspects, namely that which was called 'goalrationality' by Weber and 'instrumental reason' by the early Frankfurters. Habermas proposes, instead, a different paradigm, that of communication theory, which should allow for the analysis of those aspects of rationality which Weber allegedly did lose sight of in his study of the rationalisation of society. If attention is also focused on these latter aspects, so Habermas claims, we should arrive at far less pessimistic conclusions about the overall process of rationalisation.

We have spoken of the similarity between Habermas' view on ethical progress and eighteenth- and nineteenth-century thought on this topic. We should now hasten to stress the differences. What sets Habermas apart from these earlier thinkers is that he accepts the possibility of progress but in no way regards it as inevitable and unstoppable. When he talks of communicative competence and communicative rationality he is dealing with *possibilities*. Whether these are realised is largely a matter of often fortuitous historical circumstances, engendered by Man's contact with the environment in his effort to achieve the material reproduction of society. Here Habermas makes a distinction between the *logic* and the *dynamics* of development. This distinction is of great importance to him because it allows him to speak of *selective rationalisation* and to compare the actual course of events critically with the possible one. The logic of development concerns the possible unfolding of all aspects of rationality. However, the dynamics of development can lead to emphasis on one aspect rather than another. Habermas' main argument against Weber is that the latter identified the actual course of Western rationalisation with (the possibilities of) rationalisation as such and therefore arrived, as did indeed the early Frankfurters who largely followed Weber here, at unwarranted pessimistic conclusions about the *necessary* outcome of rationalisation. He believes also that Weber underestimated, or rather misrepresented (especially in his sociology of law), such ethical rationalisation as actually took place.

Though Habermas does not share Weber's pessimism about an alleged necessary outcome of rationalisation he nevertheless largely agrees with the latter's opinions about the loss of meaning and the loss of freedom in the contemporary world. This is because he identifies not one but two processes of rationalisation in Western history, of which the second ultimately reacts adversely on the first. These two processes of rationalisation concern, respectively, the Lifeworld and the System, in which the former stands, as far as its social dimension is concerned (there is for Habermas also a cultural and personal dimension of the Lifeworld), for the whole ensemble of human relations which is coordinated and reproduced via communicative action, and thus via the medium of language. Habermas speaks, in this context, of the *symbolic* reproduction of society. He distinguishes this from its *material* reproduction which has to do with the preservation of bodies, in the most literal sense, and which takes place through systems of action which, in modern society, have become more or less independent, mainly in the form of the subsystems market and state.

In the double process of rationalisation signalled by Habermas, the development and increasing independence of the System is originally made possible through the rationalisation of the Lifeworld, especially one aspect of this: the development of modern law. Eventually, however, as a consequence of the crisis-ridden character of the capitalist mode of production and the need to accommodate the social tensions generated by it, the expansion of the System damages the Lifeworld. Habermas calls this the colonisation of the Lifeworld.

How does this process come about? We saw that the rationalisation of the Lifeworld is expressed in the greater scope for genuine communicative action in which shared understanding, and the coordination of action based on this, is rationally motivated. We also saw that Habermas conceives, with Durkheim, of an archaic stage of social evolution in which social integration takes place through the ritual use of sacred symbols. With the growing complexity of society this integrative role is taken over by communicative action through language in a process Habermas calls the 'linguistification of the sacred'. However, the integrative role of communicative action is, with this increasing complexity, namely in the sphere of material reproduction, limited by the interpretive difficulties and possibilities for misunderstanding which the use of language as a medium for interaction always entails. Whole fields of action, namely those having to do with the market and goverment administration, eventually 'drop out of language' as it were. Steering media such as money and power take over the integrative role of language in these fields of action, which together constitute the System. There is, however, in a society based on the capitalist mode of production, an 'expansionist' tendency in the System. This tendency is triggered off by the systemic need to accommodate the tensions generated by capitalist exploitation. Because of this systemic need these steering media intrude into areas of the Lifeworld which remain vitally dependent on integration through communicative action, namely those areas which have to do with the Lifeworld's symbolic (rather than material) reproduction. By penetrating into these areas, as 'colonial overlords in a tribal society', they generate a social pathology for which the great sociologists of the past had already found various terms (alienation, anomie, loss of meaning and of freedom) but not the right analysis of its cause. This social pathology is not the *necessary* outcome of the rationalisation of the System, and therefore Habermas does not see the latter process as universally undesirable. On the contrary, to a certain extent systemic rationalisation constitutes an evolutionary gain. It only engenders social pathological phenomena in our type of society because it escapes from the normative control exercised from the Lifeworld and disturbs, in the process called 'colonisation of the Lifeworld', the latter's symbolic reproduction. Why is there so little resistance from a rationalised Lifeworld to its own 'colonisation'? Habermas sees the basic cause for this in the prevention of that global type of interpretation which is found on the level of ideology. This prevention has to do with the fragmentation of everyday consciousness which robs it of its synthetic power. Though over time an impressive amount of knowledge has been accumulated in the various spheres of science, ethics and art, this knowledge is found in the form of expert subcultures and cannot be forged into an overall perspective from which the colonisation of the Lifeworld can be effectively criticised. Fragmented consciousness has taken the place of false consciousness.

Habermas' distinction between Lifeworld and System, and that between the various types of action he links up with it, is not only of philosophical-historical, but for sociologists, also of great methodological significance. He connects action theory with systems theory, and argues that society should be 'understood' from the participant attitude of the actor as far as the Lifeworld and from the objectivating attitude of the observer as far as the System is concerned. The former activity is an exercise in communicative rationality, the latter a grasping of functional reason.

Finally, rationality is, for Habermas, also decisive for sociology as a critical discipline. The critique exercised by critical theory, in Habermas' sense, is not based on arbitrarily chosen norms but rests on the analysis, the 'reconstruction', of communicative competence. As we indicated above, this allows him to make a distinction between the logic and the dynamics of development, to compare possibilities with the actual situation. We saw above that some of his great predecessors did not make this distinction. This led, in the case of Weber, to an identification of the development of a certain aspect of rationality with the only possible course of rationalisation. The fact that he and others did so was due, so Habermas believes, to a mistaken idea of social action and a concomitant too narrow conception of rationality. We will have a closer look at this point in the following chapters.

I
The Theory in Outline

1
From the philosophy of consciousness to communication rationality: a paradigm change

One of Habermas' main concerns in the *Theory of Communicative Action* is to extricate the theory of society as a critical enterprise from a situation in which it was unable to formulate the criteria on the basis of which it could engage in critique. This theoretical bankruptcy came about because of the way it dealt with an inherited piece of theory, namely Weber's thesis on rationalisation. It is Habermas' view that the alleged theoretical shortcomings of Weber and the early Frankfurters on this point were caused by their reliance on a certain philosophical paradigm, that of the philosophy of consciousness. Thus his analysis here amounts to an argument for the replacement of this paradigm by an altogether different one, that of communication theory. Let us have a closer look at this.

We saw above that Habermas criticises Weber for identifying one specific form of rationalisation, namely that which took place over the few centuries of the development of capitalism, as its only possible form and in addition of misrepresenting to a certain extent what actually took place in this era. Habermas' criticism of this amounts at the same time to a critique of theorists such as Lukács, Horkheimer and Adorno who collectively drew on Weber here.

There were quite a few differences between the views of Horkheimer, who was the main manager of what was later called the 'Frankfurt School', as a research organisation, and those of Weber, but they agreed on the thesis that rationalisation has led to a loss of meaning, because of the breakdown of metaphysical-religious world views, and a loss of freedom. Horkheimer and Weber pointed to the same paradox: the credibility of religious and metaphysical world views declined, and with it their socially integrating force, because of the rationalisation to which they in fact owed their origin. Science could not take their place because, though it could explain the world, it could not deal with the problem of the reason for its existence and it could not understand the world of humankind as part of the cosmological order. Thus the goalrationality of science, that which Horkheimer and Adorno called instrumental reason, remained unchecked. There were no criteria on the basis of which its meaning could be queried.

Horkheimer and Weber also agreed that rationalisation led to a loss of freedom, though they explained this in different ways. Weber conceived of this in action-theoretical terms. The goalrational actions of people in the modern era were originally controlled by their moral judgment and autonomous will. But with further bureaucratisation the goalrationality of actions was ensured independently from the value-rational judgments of organisation members.

Horkheimer, however, analysed this loss of freedom in psychoanalytical rather than action-theoretical terms. According to him the control of behaviour was switched from the superego of the socialised individual to the planning agencies of social organisations. Individualisation processes found less and less support in the cultural sphere, because the cognitive instrumental rationality of economy and state marginalised cultural reproduction as irrational.

Here Horkheimer followed the views of another Marxist theorist who was strongly influenced by Weber, the Hungarian philosopher Lukács. The key term used by Lukács in this context was 'thingification' (sometimes translated as reification). He gave the widest possible application to Marx's idea that in the capitalist mode of production the social character of labour took on the appearance of being an aspect of the labour product and that in this way the social relations between people assumed the character of a relation between things. The commodity form became the predominant form of all things. This thingification was the other side of a rationalisation of action orientations which amounted to a growing predominance of instrumental reason. Mechanisation and rational calculation now also determined the way in which human beings dealt with each other and themselves. As Lukács put it:

> The transformation of the commodity relation into a thing of 'ghostly objectivity' cannot therefore content itself with the reduction of all objects for the gratification of human needs to commodities. It stamps its imprint upon the whole consciousness of man; his qualities and abilities are no longer an organic part of his personality, they are things which he can 'own' or 'dispose of' like the various objects of the

external world. And there is no natural form in which human relations can be cast, no way in which man can bring his physical and psychic 'qualities' into play without their being subjected increasingly to this reifying process. (Lukács, 1971:100)

For Lukács there was, however, a limit to this process of reification (or thingification) in the consciousness which the proletariat, on the basis of its objective situation in the historical process, developed while becoming a class for itself. The vehicle of this consciousness was not this or that individual worker, or a collection of them, but the party.

Widespread criticism of this latter point of view centered, first, on the fact that Lukács could not indicate from which standpoint outside history he could judge the historical process and, second, on the way in which actual events in allegedly socialist countries failed to bear out his views on the mission of the proletariat.

Habermas points out that Lukács did not want to put his faith in the revolutionary mechanism indicated by Marx, namely that of the growing and crisis-generating contradiction between the forces and relations of production, because he was aware of the role of science, both as a force of production and as ideology. In its latter role science identified its own mode of cognition with cognition as such. True knowledge was scientific knowledge.

Horkheimer and Adorno shared this view on the role of science as ideology but emphasised, in their account of the triumph of 'instrumental reason', that the species could only maintain itself through the domination of nature, which was concomitant with the domination of other subjects, and of humankind's own subjectivity. Hence in the application of instrumental reason what reason had to maintain, namely the human being's subjectivity, was destroyed. The exercise of instrumental reason thus became a goal in itself. There was no subjective resistance possible against this, because thought could not offer a privileged presence from which this resistance could be inspired. All thought was now regarded by Horkheimer and Adorno as, 'identifying' thought, which destroyed the uniqueness of individual things, while its conceptual strait-jackets were turned into an instrument of domination.

The bankruptcy of earlier critical theory, of which we spoke above, is found exactly on this point where, by taking its own thought to its ultimate consequence, it lost the basis for its critical enterprise. Habermas emphasises that this is not a matter of coincidence but is due to the fact that the paradigm on which it drew, the paradigm of the philosophy of consciousness, was really a blind alley for critical theory. The renewal of critical theory is thus for Habermas only possible on the basis of a paradigm change, namely to that of communication theory.

The most characteristic element of the philosophy of consciousness is that it conceives of subjective reason as regulating two relations which the subject can have to the object, namely that of *cognition*, in which the object is allegedly represented as it is, and that of *action*, in which it is produced as it should be. These functions are, moreover, perceived as only taking place within the context of the material self-maintenance of the species, which is a matter of the control and repression of nature. Thus instrumental reason is an instrument of domination against which, for early critical theory, resistance was hardly possible.

Habermas believes that critical theory can only get out of this blind alley by replacing the paradigm of the philosophy of consciousness with that of communication theory, in which not the subject-object relation (with its two elements: cognition and manipulation) but the subject-subject relation is put central. The key element is here the achievement of shared understanding of what certain acts of cognition and manipulation of objects mean. Such understanding is reached in the interpretive efforts of individuals who coordinate their action through criticisable claims to validity.

> If we assume that the human species maintains itself through the
> socially coordinated activities of its members and that this
> coordination has to be established through communication—and in
> certain central spheres through communication aimed at reaching
> agreement—then the reproduction of the species *also* requires
> satisfying the conditions of a rationality that is inherent in
> communicative action. (Habermas, 1984:I 397)

Thus the theory of society has to analyse not only instrumental action but also action based on the achievement of shared understanding, that is, communicative action. Before we have a closer look at Habermas' account of communicative action, we will briefly discuss some modern developments in the philosophy of science which seem to reinforce, from a different point of view, his insistence on the need of a paradigm change. This will enable us also to highlight the way in which we find a still rather implicit approach to this demand in an earlier period of Habermas' career.

From the beginning of his professional life Habermas has protested against what he used to call a 'positivistically truncated Reason', that is the idea that 'rational', 'scientific' procedures can only be legitimately applied to observable and quantifiable aspects of reality and that ultimately only sense impressions could be decisive in the quest for truth. His concern has been throughout to widen this rather too limiting concept of rationality. He originally tried to do this by making a distinction between various types of knowledge (empirical-analytical, historical-hermeneutical and emancipatory knowledge), each of which had to do with different types of activities (labour, interaction and emancipation) and was allegedly guided by a different fundamental interest. These constructive attempts went hand in hand with a critique of what Habermas used to call 'scientism', that is, science's view of itself, not as one *form* of cognition but as cognition as such. To accept this self-image of science would, for Habermas, amount to the banning of important questions outside the realm of rational discourse, namely also those which have to do with the problem of what constitutes right action. Widening the concept of rationality meant to Habermas also the acknowledgment that theoretical discourse, centering on questions of truth about the objective world, was not the only form of rational discourse. Beside this one had to recognise, among other things, the possibility of practical discourse, which focused on questions of rightness concerning the social world. Habermas' attempts to broaden the concept of rationality have been increasingly couched in communication-theoretical rather than epistemological terms and it is a matter of dispute to what extent he has, in doing so, abandoned his earlier views. However this may be, one cannot say that he has given up his resistance against positivism, the most extreme form of which could be found in the 'logical empiricism' of the so-called Vienna Circle. This philosophy had a very definite idea of reality and the way we get to know it. Reality allegedly consisted of objectively given and causally linked things and events. Knowledge was, in this view, a relation between, on the one hand, objectively given reality and, on the other, the knowing subject. Truth was a matter of correspondence between propositions formulated by these knowing subjects, and this reality.

Thus the knowing subject was regarded as a 'solitary ego' who could have, basically, only two sorts of relations with the objects confronting him or her: s/he could *know* them and s/he could *manipulate* them. Each subject had a sensory apparatus which allowed him/her to know the object directly and to come up with observational statements. The knowledge of reality was based on the agreement in these observational statements. Thus, in this view of our processes of cognition, the subject-object relation was made central, as it was during a considerable part of the history of modern philosophy since Descartes. In the nineteenth century the Cartesian paradigm came under fire from various sides. The details of this story are beyond the scope of this book. Let us confine ourselves to the observation, already made above, that it survived in this century, in its most extreme form, in 'logical empiricism'. We saw that Habermas called this philosophical paradigm the 'philosophy of consciousness'. For this philosophy the quality of knowledge, and rationality as such, is ultimately dependent on the quality of subject-object relations and the observational statements based on these. By contrast Habermas proposes, as we saw, another philo-sophical paradigm, that of communication theory, in which know-ledge is, ultimately, dependent on subject-subject relations.

We can perhaps best explain what this implies by a short sketch of those post-World War II developments in the philosophy of science which have had most influence on sociology (even though today Habermas himself does not present his views in this context). What is important here is that these developments have undermined the neopositivism of the Vienna circle and the subject-object paradigm on which it was based, *and that this has happened through a 'sociologisation' and 'historisation' of knowledge in general.*

The positivist view that the accumulation of knowledge takes place in a process in which ultimately observational statements, formulated with the help of more or less crucial experiments, were decisive in the acceptance or rejection of theories was challenged in the following way. First, a fairly general consensus came about that there are no such things as theory-free observational statements. Any such statement is couched in terms which imply again theory-derived hypotheses. Even in the statement 'here is a glass of water', for instance, such terms as 'glass' and 'water' refer to hypotheses about the behaviour of certain things. Therefore, as Karl Popper has indicated, the acceptance of a so-called basic statement depends on the provisional and revocable consensus of the 'forum' of scientists (cf. Popper, 1972:94–95, 1965:387). But if this is so the problem how, and under which conditions, this consensus is arrived at becomes a fundamental one. And this is, at least in part, a sociological and historical problem.

This has been taken further. If theories are falsified, even though provisionally, with the help of basic statements, which are them-selves impregnated with theory, this latter theory is given (even though, again, provisionally) a privileged status. Which theories have or have not, in a certain period, a privileged status is not so much a matter of the *logic of science but of its sociology and history.* This insight was the basis of what, according to some, is the Copernican turn in the postwar philosophy of science—a turn which has been identified with the name of Thomas Kuhn.

For the social sciences this upheaval in the philosophy of science has had the following consequences. First, it has led to a deepened suspicion against naive positivistic views in which the process of cognition is made dependent on the (correct) observation of an objective reality which can be approached from the outside as it were. Second, and related to this, the 'sociologisation' and 'historisation' of knowledge has been extended to sociology itself. The most general effect of the 'Kuhnian turn' in sociology is the by now widespread conviction of the relativity of all knowledge and the (somewhat less widespread) belief in the untenability of the concept of truth. Indeed, in sociology the opinions which filtered through from the philosophy of science fell, especially in Germany, into a readily prepared ground. Suspicion of positivism was linked here to the conviction that the object of sociology should not merely be observed and explained from the outside, but 'understood' from the inside. Habermas has, in this respect at least, shown himself to be a true scion of German sociology by not only taking the 'Kuhnian turn' to its ultimate consequence but also by fitting the insights involved here in a theory of rationality which goes far beyond mere preoccupation with the realm of science.

The paradigm change Habermas proposes, though in his case arrived at by a different path, has a direct bearing on the central problem here. In his recent *Twelve Lectures Concerning the Philosophical Discourse on Modernity* Habermas asks where 'Reason' should be situated after the 'historisation' and 'sociologisation' of the cognitive process. How can we deal with the paradox that it is Reason itself which has led us to the acknowledgement of its historical and social limitations, and yet, in the very process of positing this, seems to want to escape from these? If it can gain certainty about its limitations, it should be able to gain certainty about other things—but that again would lead to a denial of its limitations, and so on.

Habermas' view is that Reason will, after the development in philosophy since Kant, no longer be able to reserve a sanctuary for itself in some privileged subject: be it the 'transcendental', unhistorical subject of Kant's 'pure reason' or the global subject behind Hegel's picture of Reason's 'externalisation' and reabsorption in history, or the privileged historical subject (the working class) of Marxist thought. Reason, says Habermas, is not to be situated in any one particular subject at all but rather in subject-subject *relations*. Rationality is 'communicative rationality'. This means that, for the analysis of the evolution of society, the knowledge and the putting at our disposal of an objectivated nature are no longer the central phenomena needing explanation. Rather it is the intersubjectivity of shared understanding which now becomes the core phenomenon.

> The focus of investigation thereby shifts from cognitive-instrumental rationality to communicative rationality. And what is paradigmatic for the latter is not the relation of a solitary subject to something in the objective world that can be represented and manipulated, but the intersubjective relation that speaking and acting subjects take up when they come to an understanding with one another about something. (Habermas, 1984a:I 392)

Habermas' idea that it is subject–subject relations rather than subject–object relations which are at the heart of Reason's appearance in history does not imply that a formerly rational preserve is now opened up to the irrationality of daily life. Nor does it mean that the idea of truth has been given up. On the contrary. Rather than stressing that the realm of rationality is not as vast as we once thought it was, Habermas has emphasised that it is, in fact, far more extensive than most of us were originally inclined to believe. Rather than accepting that the arbitrariness allegedly found in the realm of norms and values has now also penetrated the realm of science, he has emphasised that, potentially, norms too can be a subject of rational discourse, as can be inner states and feelings. In short, Habermas has argued for a far broader concept of rationality. This broader concept allows him to escape from the paradoxical situation in which philosophy had manoeuvred itself, a situation in which Reason came to a conclusion about its historical and social character which seemed to deny its capacity to come to any conclusion at all. Habermas' conception of rationality *accepts* its historical character by seeing the expression, in history, of a 'logic of development' (to be distinguished, as we have already seen, from the 'dynamics of development') which is based, ultimately, on the communicative rationality which pervades communicative action. This communicative rationality, though expressed in a historical context, transcends history for those who express it in their actions.

On this particular point Habermas has not changed his opinion from the beginning of his academic career, even though it is only at a later stage that he has worked out the sociological implications of this view. We are dealing here with what he has called himself the central intuition informing his work. To put it succinctly: for Habermas being human is bound up with a *certain* use of language. We saw that he argues that the human species maintains itself by the socially coordinated activities of its members. This coordination must be brought about through communication, and in central areas through communication which aims at shared agreement. Language plays a vital role in this. Habermas stresses that, otherwise than has been thought until recently, the capacity to formulate propositions representing facts in the objective world is not a human monopoly. Modern ethology has learned from experiments with chimpanzees that this capacity goes beyond the human realm, as, of course, does the capacity to make an appeal to others and to express inner feelings. The typically human element in language use is to be found in its communicative character (Habermas, 1985a:363). The human use of language implies a common endeavour to achieve consensus in a situation in which all participants are free to have their say and have equal chances to express their views. Thus there is in language an inbuilt thrust for the achievement of what Habermas calls the 'ideal speech situation', in which discourse can fully unfold its potential for rationality. As he said about the use of language in his inaugural oration: 'With the first sentence used the intention to reach a general and uncompelled consensus is pronounced unmistakably' (Habermas, 1970:163). This does not of course mean that the situation in which language can fully unfold its potential for rationality will in fact be reached, but it does mean that the process of communicative action, though always taking place in a historical context, also depends on a factor which goes beyond the bounds of the immediate historical situation. This factor is found in the claim for the validity of the reasons which induce people to take their particular share in communicative action. In such claims no historical limitation is recognised since they are based on the (implicit) view that their validity should be accepted by anyone capable of judgment who is free to use it, whether in the past, present or future. The idea of rationally motivated shared understanding—and rational motivation implies the total lack of compulsion or manipulation—is built into the very reproduction of social life, so Habermas claims. The symbolic reproduction of society is based on the 'counterfactual' ideal of the 'ideal speech situation', which is characterised by 'communicative symmetry' and a compulsion-free consensus. Habermas does not however, as we saw, present history as a process of unstoppable progress to this situation (Habermas, 1985a:375, 1982:277). We have referred already to the distinction he makes between the logic and the dynamics of development. The latter term refers to the many external circumstances which influence the process of the unfolding of language's potential for rationality, and the development of a situation in which it can be expressed.

Before we have a look at Habermas' sketch of the logic of development we will elaborate on his views about communicative rationality as expressed in communicative action.

2
Action, communicative rationality and the Lifeworld

We saw in the previous chapter that one of Habermas' main objections to the 'philosophy of consciousness' is that its too narrow concept of rationality prevents adequate analysis of the historical development called 'rationalisation', and the pathology of the modern era this ultimately leads to. This limited idea of rationality is, in the case of Weber, found on what is for sociology the most basic conceptual level, that of action. Weber emphasised the 'goal-rational' aspects of action and therefore, Habermas maintains, incurred the loss of that wider concept of rationality which is gained when social action is seen for what it allegedly is, namely communicative action taking place on the basis of communicative rationality. As we will see later, it is because Habermas operates with this wider concept of rationality that he can present a perspective of development which is rather different from the very pessimistic one offered by Weber (and in his wake the early Frankfurters).

Of course, the 'central intuition' informing Habermas' work from the beginning has been that the fact that humankind can use language is at the basis of its capacity for rationality. This competence is expressed in communicative action which is oriented to shared understanding and in which language is used as a medium to reach this. Let us have a closer look then at Habermas' analysis of communicative action, and later, his account of the role of language in this.

First we will look back at Weber's definition of social action: 'Social action is that action which, as far as its intended meaning is concerned, refers to other people's behaviour and remains oriented to this while it proceeds.' This definition of action is, to Habermas, not discriminatory enough because it glosses over the fact that a) social action can be oriented to quite different things such as the

13

achievement of shared understanding or that of merely personal success and b) that interaction is *coordinated* in basically different ways. Weber's concept of social action has mainly to do with a specific kind of action orientation. Habermas says that this is a consequence of Weber's dependence on the philosophy of consciousness, which led him to give a central place in his analysis to the isolated actor. The aspect of the achievement of shared understanding as an intersubjective activity, and with it the coordination of action, was thus lost sight of. It is only, Habermas believes, by taking this latter dimension into account that we can gain a precise concept of communicative action and with it a wider concept of rationality which includes its communicative as well as its instrumental aspect. This has momentous consequences for the analysis of rationalisation. A model of action which directs attention to goalrationality rather than communicative rationality will also focus on the former type of rationality in rationalisation and hence lead to what Habermas regards as the one-sided and pessimistic conclusions of Weber and the early Frankfurters.

For Habermas the correct analysis of society and its developmental tendencies starts at the bottom, as it were, with the right idea of social action, which focuses on the intersubjective achievement of shared understanding.

Let us first try to look at the difference in action orientations between communicative and non-communicative action by way of an example. Imagine you have rented a room somewhere in the cheaper quarters of a great city which happen to contain the red-light district. After you have been living there for a while your landlord sees more lucrative uses for your room and increases the rent drastically in order to induce you to vacate it. But you don't yield. However, you have a fiancé who is also convinced that you should find some other place, because he feels that you endanger your (and his) reputation by living there and/or that you are actually in danger when you return home late etc. He discusses this matter with you frequently. Now you might or might not heed his arguments, but you can see quite clearly the difference between your friend's and your landlord's activities on this score (even though these both fall under Weber's definition of social action). The main difference Habermas would see between these and similar cases is that, in the first example, that of the landlord, who tries to get you out by increasing the rent, action is oriented to egoistic calculations of success, whereas in the second case, that of your worried fiancé, the latter's action is oriented to reaching shared understanding. Habermas calls action oriented to success *strategic action* when it is oriented to subjects rather than objects (if it is oriented to the latter it is called *instrumental action*). Strategic action is judged along one particular dimension of rationality. It can be 'appraised from the standpoint of the efficiency of influencing the decisions of rational opponents' (Habermas, 1982:264). Action oriented to reaching shared understanding Habermas calls *communicative action*, and in the following definition we find both the mode of its action orientation and coordination specified: communicative action 'is that form of social interaction in which the plans of action of different actors are co-ordinated through an exchange of communicative acts, that is, through a use of language (or corresponding non-verbal expressions) oriented towards reaching understanding' (1982:234). To reach understanding means here that the partners in interaction set out, and manage, to convince each other, so that their action is coordinated on the basis of motivation through reason.

Motivation through reason does not always require the use of language in explicit argument; in fact, this will generally not be the case. We should also emphasise here that Habermas does not say that the participants in communicative action have no individual ends, but only that if these are pursued under the condition of a communicatively produced consensus regarding the given situation they have to make use of language in a manner oriented to reaching understanding (1982:237). When coordination has been reached, in whatever fashion, actors perform on the basis of this, goal-directed actions 'that exhibit . . . the structure of purposive activity'.

Habermas does not identify speech with action; rather speech provides the mechanism for the coordination of communicative action. This makes it quite different from strategic action which is oriented, as we saw, to egocentric calculations of success and coordinated on the basis of the complementarity of interests, such as we can find, for instance, in a market situation or a bureaucratically structured arrangement. Since in our present social economic order these are characterised by structured inequality, the fact that coordination takes place via a complementarity of interests does not imply that motivation is based on reason, the conviction that justice is being done all around. It can be in somebody's interest to avoid punishment or to accept an offer of unequal exchange. The essential point is that in strategic action ego influences the choice situation of alter not through criticisable claims couched in language (Habermas calls these 'validity claims') but by 'sanctions or gratifications, force or money' (1982:269). The motivation for action is *empirical*.

Thus in communicative action the coordination of action is not based on an a priori normative consensus (as, for instance, Parsons pictures it to be) but on 'the participants' own fallible accomplishments of reaching understanding'. We spoke above of the various dimensions of rationality inherent in communicative action. Let us now have a closer look at these. The rationality inherent in communicative action has more than one aspect. The essential element for Habermas here is the recognition that the validity claims exchanged in communicative action refer to different 'worlds'.

Here then we encounter the other major point in his rejection of the 'philosophy of consciousness'. He protests not only against its epistemology (that is its views on the origin and nature of knowledge, based on the picture of an isolated subject encountering a separate object) but also against its ontology (its views on the nature of reality). The ontology of the 'philosophy of consciousness' is, Habermas asserts, just too narrow; that this has not been recognised is because action has been seen, quite generally, in the wrong light. In communicative action the use of language is, as we saw, oriented towards reaching shared understanding. Such language use requires the exchange of criticisable validity claims. Habermas asserts that these claims refer to more than one world. There are claims to truth, referring to an 'objective world of existing states of affairs' (which is the only world recognised among the most positivistic adherents of the 'philosophy of consciousness'). There are also, however, claims to (normative) rightness referring to the 'social world of legitimately regulated interpersonal relations' and claims to sincerity or authenticity referring to each person's 'own subjective world of experiences to which he or she has privileged access'.

How should we picture these worlds? Habermas speaks here of *formal* world concepts. Hence these 'worlds' do not constitute separate domains, like geographical territories with clearly marked boundaries, but rather forms under which we organise our attempts to reach a common definition of the situation via language. Since we saw above that epistemology is for Habermas not a matter of subject–object but of subject–subject relations, it can cause no surprise that for each of these worlds he specifies a different subject-subject relation. Language, with its range of different pronouns, points the way here. When we look at the different validity claims embodied in speech acts, says Habermas, we have to postulate worlds 'not only for the "object", which confronts us in the position of third person, but also for "the normative", to which we feel obliged in the position of addressee, and for the "subjective", which we, in the position of first person, reveal or hide for a public' (Habermas, 1985a:365).

Let us after this fairly abstract disquisition return to our example in which we imagined you to be hounded by your landlord and beseeched by your fiancé. Your fiancé is worried, and he discusses the situation with you in that context. Is your reputation endangered by the fact that you live in a certain neighbourhood? Do you really run a risk when you return home late at night? Can he, your fiancé, convey to you how bad he feels about the whole situation? You will notice that your fiancé is, in the 'validity claims' which have to do with these questions, indeed referring to each of the three worlds mentioned in the previous paragraph: the 'social world' (nice girls should not live in slummy red-light districts), the 'objective world' (this place is dangerous at night) and the 'subjective world' (I feel bad about all this). Note too that in the validity claims referring to the 'social world' two questions could be basically asked: is this the norm? (you could argue that your fiancé is very old-fashioned and simply not aware of the general shift in attitude on these matters) and: is this norm right? (you could agree that most people would hold that nice girls should not live in red-light districts but that they are simply wrong in holding this). In any case, the upshot of the discussion could be that you are convinced by your fiancé's arguments and together you start packing your things; in other words you engage in the 'purposive activity' which, Habermas says, is based on the coordination reached via the exchange of validity claims. On the other hand, you might convince your fiancé that he has the wrong view of the situation and he might decide to help you in your resistance against the landlord. Essential in both cases (you coming to your fiancé's views or he coming to yours) is that action is taken on the basis of a definition of the situation agreed on by both parties and reached in a process in which 'validity claims' are exchanged and which is characterised by what Habermas calls 'communicative rationality'. Before we discuss this latter concept we should have a close look at a related one: that of communicative competence.

Habermas maintains that agents can themselves make, intuitively and implicitly, the distinction between strategic and communicative action which the theorist makes explicitly. The competence involved here he calls 'communicative competence'. It is one of those competences which he identifies with the concept of personality. 'By the concept of personality', he writes, 'I understand those competences which make a subject capable of speech and action, that is able to participate in processes in which shared understanding is reached, maintaining at the same time his or her own identity' (Habermas, 1984b:594–95). He maintains that such competences can be established in a 'reconstructive science', which aims at finding out the 'depth structure' of a symbolical order, in this case the rules which are at the basis of linguistic communication and which competent speakers (that is speakers with communicative competence) can apply though they would not be able to spell them out.

The term communicative competence has been coined in analogy with the term 'linguistic competence' which was first used in a specific sense by the American linguist Noam Chomsky. Habermas' 'communicative competence' and Chomsky's 'linguistic competence' are rather different. Yet if we have a closer look at what Chomsky meant by his concept we might also come a bit nearer to the meaning of the term used by Habermas.

Chomsky created the term 'linguistic competence' to point to, among other things, the remarkable discrepancy between knowledge and experience in the use of language. A language consists of a great but *limited* number of elements. Yet anyone who has a command of that language can produce and understand an *unlimited* number of sentences and also judge whether a certain sequence of expressions is in accordance with the rules governing the use of that language. Hence the competent speaker knows more than s/he can have learned in the contact with his or her linguistic environment; this is especially conspicuous in the use of a language by children. Chomsky used the term 'linguistic competence' to indicate the implicit command of an abstract system of rules in the use of language and he assumed that this command is based on an inborn linguistic apparatus. Note that the knowledge of how to apply the rules governing language use is not based on the ability to state explicitly what these rules are. In most cases people would not have conscious knowledge of these rules. This is, again, most conspicuous in children's use of language.

Habermas has his objections to Chomsky's concept, but these are of no direct concern to us. What is important here is that he means by 'communicative competence', in relation to social situations, something similar to what Chomsky means by 'linguistic competence' in relation to (monological) language situations. As we saw, 'linguistic competence' consists of the ability to follow, more or less unconsciously, certain rules in the production of sentences. 'Communicative competence' also consists of the ability to follow rules, but this time not rules for the production of sentences but, rather, for the use of these sentences in utterances in social situations. It is these 'rules' which also underlie the distinctions we make 'intuitively' between one type of action and another, between the various validity claims (claims to truth, to rightness, to sincerity and authenticity), and the worlds they refer to (the objective world, the social world, the inner world of subjective experience). Thus a theory of communicative competence wants, among other things, to reconstruct the rules on the basis of which the transformation of a grammatically correct sentence into a social utterance can take place.

We should keep in mind here that it is communicative competence, this 'anthropologically basic structure', which allows us to give scope to the various dimensions of communicative rationality. Thanks to communicative rationality various agents can, through the non-compelling force of discursive reason, make sure of the unity of the objective world and the intersubjectivity of their Lifeworld (Habermas,1984:I 10). Language is the vehicle for all this. Communicative rationality is contained in the structure of human speech as such.

In order to make this clear we have to go back to some of Habermas' earlier work, notably his essay on the theory of communicative competence (1971). He maintains in this article that any genuine initiation of and participation in communication is based on the supposition that, in principle, the shared understanding which communicative action aims at can, if need be, be reached by switching from one level of communication to another, namely from communicative action to discourse. Thus there are two forms of communication involved here: communicative action, which is communication embedded in a specific situation, and discourse, which is communication in which all non-verbal elements have been bracketed as much as possible. The possibility of switching from one level of action to another implies that the validity claims offered on the level of action can in principle be discussed, and confirmed or rejected, on the level of discourse. The supposition that we can always, if need be, switch from the level of communicative action to that of discourse is 'counterfactual' in the sense that genuine communication must be based on it, though we might experience in practice that this switch cannot always be effectively realised.

There is yet another supposition involved in the initiation of and participation in communication, namely the idea that discourse can lead to a 'true' consensus rather than just a forced one or one which is proclaimed only for the sake of peace. The achievement of a true consensus requires the possibility of a situation called by Habermas, at this stage in his publicistic career, the 'ideal speech situation'. Raising claims implies the possibility that they can, if need be, be discussed and this again, implies that in principle this discussion can take place in an 'ideal speech situation' which is characterised by a symmetrical distribution of chances to engage in it for all participants in discourse. As Habermas says:

> It now turns out to be the case that the model of pure communicative action does not only require, as shown, the possibility of discourse but rather that, conversely, the possibilities of discourse cannot be conceived of independently from the conditions for pure communicative action . . . These determinations mutually interpret each other and define together a form of life which gives validity to the maxim that, when we engage in communication to conduct a discourse, and continue this only long enough, a consensus must come about which is, by its nature, a true consensus. (1971:139)

Thus communicative competence is the competence to achieve rationality with the means available to us in language, which, if used, are steering us in the way of reason. Those linguistic means do not only presuppose the possibility of discourse but also indicate what type of discourse we should engage in if communication is switched to that level.

If a claim about the 'objective world' is a matter of dispute the discourse we engage in will be 'theoretical'. If the disputed claim refers to the social world our discourse will be 'practical'. The claim concerned refers in the latter case not to *truth*, as is the matter with a claim about the objective world, but to *rightness*. How can we with the help of language indicate the world we are specifically referring to in our validity claim and, accordingly, the type of discourse we have to engage in if the claim is disputed? Which functions of language are involved here? That language *can* have various functions is not a new view. To mention only one example, the German psychologist Karl Bühler had already made this clear more than half a century ago. He distinguished between language's *cognitive* function (the linguistic sign then serves as a symbol and is related to objects and matters of fact), its *expressive* function (the sign then serves as a symbol for the inner experiences of the sender) and the *appeal* function (the sign then serves as a symbol in an appeal, of some kind or other, to the hearer).

How can language have these various functions? Let us consider in this context, as Habermas does, the views of the English philosopher John Austin, who can be regarded as the founding father of the theory of the 'speech act'. The term itself indicates what he was driving at here. Utterances in language constitute an 'action'. They do not only describe something but they bring something about. In order to indicate the descriptive aspect of utterances Austin used the term 'constatives'. He used another well-chosen term to indicate that aspect of the utterance which refers to the speaker doing something: 'performatives'. What should we think of here? Think of utterances like 'I promise that I will not stay out late' or 'I warn you that I will not accept that again'. These utterances imply an action namely, respectively, the 'making' of a promise or the 'issuing' of a warning.

Thus Austin emphasised that an utterance stands for various actions which he called 'locutionary' and 'illocutionary' acts. The term 'locutionary' refers to the fact that in the utterance we state a proposition which has a certain 'sense'. But beside that we perform, with the utterance, an action: we express satisfaction, issue a warning or order, make a promise etc. Thus 'illocutions' are what we do in saying things. Austin believed that illocutions can usually be made explicit with the help of the term 'hereby': I hereby promise you, I hereby warn you etc.

The philosopher John Searle has built further on this. He made a distinction between an illocutionary act and the propositional contents of an illocutionary act. These could vary independently. The same proposition could fit into quite different illocutionary acts.

The main point Habermas emphasises here is that it is quite clear from these analyses that language does not just have a cognitive function. It does not merely serve to represent things in the objective world, as the allegedly faulty epistemology of the 'philosophy of consciousness', with its subject–object dichotomy, would suggest it does. We saw that Habermas not only objects to the epistemology of the philosophy of consciousness but also to its ontology, which he finds too narrow. Beside the 'objective world of existing states of affairs' he distinguished, as we saw, two other formal world concepts, namely those of the 'social world of legitimately regulated interpersonal relations' and each person's 'own subjective world of inner experiences'. Thus he recognises three worlds which we could simply call the objective, the social and the subjective world.

Habermas' proposal now is to 'radicalise' linguistic philosophy in the sense that its ontological assumptions are changed as well (1984a:I 278). The recognition of other modes of linguistic usage, which is already found in this philosophy, should be expanded into that of different types of validity claims and their reference to specific worlds. He proposes, in addition, to see the illocutionary role of the speech act, not as an irrational power in opposition to the validity-bestowing propositional part (to use Searle's term), but as that component which specifies which validity claim a speaker raises with his/her utterance, how s/he raises it and for what s/he raises it.

Let us illustrate this latter point by taking the simple proposition, 'you will not find yourself alone'. Depending on the context, I might with this sentence provide a description of 'the objective world'. The person I am speaking to wants to spend a quiet afternoon on the beach, but it is magnificent weather and I make it clear to her that there will be quite a few other people on the beach. I might also, however, come up with a demand referring, in the process, to the social world. The person I am speaking to is planning to take her dog to the beach and I am telling her that she shouldn't do this because there might be people at the beach who will rightly take exception to this. Finally, I might make a promise with this simple proposition, referring, in the process, to the subjective world of my own inner feelings. The person I am speaking to is not planning to take her dog to the beach at all but, on the contrary, to point out to dog owners, whose dogs make a nuisance of themselves at the beach, that these dogs are not allowed there. I am then referring with the proposition 'you will not find yourself alone' to my own firm intention to support her.

Thus my proposition can refer to three different worlds, the three worlds Habermas has distinguished and which we indicated above, depending on the illocutionary part of the speech act. If this illocutionary part would have to be put into words (which is not always necessary because the context might make clear enough what it is) the sentences would have been: I know that you will not find yourself alone (objective world); I tell you not to go because you will not find yourself alone (social world); and I promise you that you will not find yourself alone (subjective world).

Habermas has also drawn on linguistic philosophy to show the genuine distinction in the use of language in communicative action, when all partners in interaction are oriented to reaching shared understanding, and its use in interaction, in which at least one of the agents is oriented to the egoistic calculation of results. He has endeavoured to show that the latter use is 'parasitic' on the former.

Let us, in order to clarify this point, return to our example of you living in a certain neighbourhood and your fiancé pointing out that you should not live there, because of the risks inherent in this situation, both as far as your reputation and your safety are concerned. Now it could well be that he just makes a show of discussing these claims, and trying to seek shared understanding, but that his real aim is quite different. It could be, for instance, that he wants to frighten you out of this particular house because the room adjoining yours has been rented by a fellow with whose attractions he does not care to compete. So here we have an example of action which, at first sight, looks communicative but, is in fact, strategic. In order to elucidate the characteristic features of such interaction Habermas makes use of Austin's distinction between 'illocutions' and 'perlocutions'. Let us have a closer look at this.

We saw that with a locutionary act the speaker performs an action while he is saying something (making a promise, issuing a warning etc.). Normally, the illocutionary part of the speech act allows the addition of the word 'hereby' (hereby I promise you, hereby I command). This is not possible with the perlocutionary act because what the speaker wants there is to have a certain effect on the listener. He wants to persuade him or her, or to frighten or embarrass. Obviously s/he cannot say 'Hereby I embarrass you. . .'. This surface distinction points to a deeper one. The locutionary and illocutionary aspect of a speech act should be clear from the manifest meaning of what is said. That is not so with the perlocutionary aspect. The speaker has a more or less hidden goal and the perlocutionary effects of the speech act remain, as Austin concluded, external to the meaning of what has been said. Whether such a perlocutionary effect comes about depends on a great many other causes, which do not have directly to do with the speech act itself, for instance, to return to our example, whether you, the person living in the red-light district, are easily frightened. It is because of this that Habermas says that the process of 'reaching an understanding' on the basis of speech acts, that is to say communicative action, is exclusively a matter of illocutionary acts, and that the occurrence of perlocutionary effects is a sign that the speech acts concerned really fit within the complex of strategic action. Illocutionary aims can be reached by stating them openly, thus they can be read from the speech act itself. This is not the case with perlocutionary aims. In our example your fiancé cannot state his perlocutionary aim openly without sabotaging it. He cannot say, 'I want to frighten you . . .'. The British philosopher Strawson, to whom Habermas refers on this point, saw in this matter of the openness of the illocutionary aim and the hiddenness of the perlocutionary one the right criterion for their distinction.

It is because of considerations such as these that Habermas calls perlocutions covered strategic actions even though they might be accompanied by a great deal of argument. The speech acts used in this context are 'parasitic' on those which are oriented to shared understanding. In genuine communicative action it is not so that one of the participants has a hidden goal which he or she pursues regardless of what emerges during interaction (cf. Habermas 1984a:I 295). Illocutionary aims can be stated openly and can change during communicative action because agents keep orienting themselves towards each other's validity claims. In genuine communicative action all agents follow illocutionary aims and only those. Interactions involving validity claims in which at least one participant aims at perlocutionary effects are, to Habermas, linguistically mediated concealed strategic action. This latter form of strategic action should be distinguished from linguistically mediated open strategic action, such as, for instance, 'simple imperatives', which we will deal with in the next chapter.

The distinction between strategic and communicative action does not exhaust the realm of action. From an early stage Habermas has insisted on the importance of the distinction between labour and interaction. In his earlier work he made this distinction in the context of his discussion of humankind's exchange with nature. On the one hand, the human being has to subject nature, in the most efficient way, to its needs. Here Habermas saw the necessity of goalrational action via the medium of labour. On the other hand it has, according to him, to be recognised that this process of the subjection of nature is a social one. The appropriate mode of action here is communicative action via the medium of language. In *The Theory of Communicative Action* his earlier distinction of action types re-emerges as that between, on the one hand, instrumental action and, on the other, strategic and communicative action. Instrumental action is directed towards objects, strategic and communicative action towards subjects. Instrumental action, Habermas claims, follows technical rules 'and can be appraised from the standpoint of the efficiency of goal-oriented intervention in the physical world' (1982:263). To return, and now for the last time, to our example of your precarious tenancy of a room, your fiancé can express his concern about your safety by putting an extra lock on your door. His action on the lock is instrumental, though it is, in this case, taken in a clearly social context.

To sum up, if we present Habermas' concepts of action schematically we obtain the following diagram:

	Action	
	Oriented to results	Oriented to shared understanding
Social	Strategic	Communicative
Non-social	Instrumental	

Habermas has, as we saw, endeavoured to entrench rationality at the level of sociology's most basic concept, that of action, and of its most basic thematic question, that of the reproduction of society. The reproduction of the species, says Habermas, which requires in central areas coordination of action through communication aimed at reaching agreement, also requires that the conditions for the rationality inherent in communicative action are fulfilled (1984a:I 397). What are these conditions? We saw that a basic one was that communicative action takes place via validity claims which can, if need be, be criticised in discourse. Language contains the means to specify to which world in particular a validity claim refers and, accordingly, which type of discourse we should engage in if the claim is disputed. We have pointed out before that this distinction in types of discourse is related to the recognition of the various dimensions of rationality (rather than just the one aspect, that of goalrationality, emphasised by Weber and the early Frankfurters) and with it the different aspects of rationalisation.

3
Interpretive understanding and the Lifeworld

We saw in the previous chapter that Habermas has, with the help of the philosophy of language, specified the wider notion of rationality of which the conception and defence has been central to most of his theoretical endeavours. He has demonstrated how rationality is operative in the most basic form of social action, namely communicative action which is coordinated, as we saw, 'through a use of language or corresponding non-verbal expressions oriented towards reaching understanding'. However, thus far we have been talking of communicative action exclusively in terms of speech acts, and the use of these in discourse, and have perhaps created the impression that Habermas pictures society as some kind of large-scale debating club. That is, of course, not his intention. Apart from the fact, which he draws attention to himself, that in everyday communicative practice utterances are often not in explicit speech, or have no verbal form at all, what he is really looking at is not the communication in itself but its coordinating effect on subsequent action. The specific question is thus: how can communication have action-coordinating effects. This is, according to Habermas, because a commonly reached definition of the situation, in relation to the three worlds he distinguishes, does not hang in the air but has implications for action. How can that be? In order to analyse this further we should first look at what the coordination of action in communicative action implies. There are three elements here which are linked together: the listener reacts to a claim presented in a speech act by (a) understanding its meaning, (b) taking a 'yes' or 'no' position to it and (c) if the former is the case by following this up with action in accordance with conventionally established action obligations (if s/he takes a 'no' position the interaction can be switched off or changed into discourse in which both speaker and listener can change their positions). What unites these three elements?

Let us first look at what understanding the meaning of an utterance implies from a sociological point of view. We understand a speech act, says Habermas, when we know that the speaker is able and willing to come up with convincing reasons, and if necessary to defend these, for his or her validity claim. It is the fact that this is warranted which provides binding force to an illocutionary act and which makes it have a coordinating effect on the action following communication (Habermas, 1984:I 297–302).

Let us take an example. If you are walking down the street and somebody behind you shouts ('stop',) wildly waving his arms in the process, you might say to the person next to you, 'I don't understand what that fellow is on about'. What you are then actually saying is that you do not see how he can offer any convincing reasons for his request or order. However, when you are on the beach and on the verge of going into the water and somebody shouts ('stop') and you detect, on looking around, that he is obviously a lifesaver (he is standing next to the wheel with the rope) you understand very well what this man is on about. The difference between the first and the second case is that, in the latter, you know the speaker can offer reasons for his request. These will have to do with dangerous undertows, or a recently spotted group of sharks, or whatever.

We can vary this example by having a policeman, rather than a lifesaver, ordering you to stop. In this case you might initially not have the slightest idea why you are ordered to do so, but you stop because you know that this policeman has, either directly or indirectly, control over certain negative sanctions. Your acceptance of his 'speech act' is motivated 'empirically' rather than, as was the case with the lifesaver's speech act, 'rationally'. The policeman might, if his order is challenged, exercise his control over sanctions; the lifesaver might, in a similar situation, come up with arguments. This difference provides the basis for Habermas' distinction between 'simple imperatives' and 'normatively authorised requests', and that between 'empirical' and 'rational' motivation. There is also a similarity between our last two examples; you 'understood' the order to stop because you had a grasp of the 'warrants' behind it, even though these were of a different nature. In our first example, that of the man wildly waving his arms and shouting at you, you could not think of any warrants, any reason why the order should be acceptable to you, and thus you did not understand.

To take another example, provided by Habermas himself, if a steward requests a passenger to extinguish her cigarette during the landing of an airplane the passenger can only take a 'no' position in the form of criticism of this request, which is countered by arguments from the steward, who could refer to the relevant regulations. The passenger can then criticise the regulations, for instance by doubting their legality or by saying that they make no sense. In most cases, however, she will simply respond to the steward's request by putting the cigarette out. The steward can warrant that, if necessary, his claim can be defended with arguments which will stand up to the criticism of the passenger. It is, again, the fact that this can be warranted which makes the listener 'understand' the request and which rationally motivates her to follow it up. Thus this is the element which, according to Habermas, has action-coordinating effects. It is clear that we have a different situation when the speech act consists of an imperative which does not offer a criticisable validity claim and which owes its action-coordinating effect to the fact that it is linked with a potential for sanctions, that is the implicit threat of violence or the promise of a reward.

In the instance given above we were dealing with a 'regulative speech act' referring to the social world. Speech acts which refer to the objective world Habermas calls 'constatives', and those referring to the internal world 'expressives'. What does the understanding of an expressive speech act such as, for example, 'I hate chicken' imply? It implies, says Habermas, knowing the conditions under which the speaker says what he means, that is can warrant that his further behaviour is consistent with his claim (a person who hates chicken normally does not go to buy his lunch at a fried chicken place). Thus the truthfulness of his claim is, in the first place, sustained by the consistency of his behaviour which can be discussed in argument. Conversely, a wife who claims to care about a chicken-hating husband does not serve this bird for dinner every night. Her expressive utterances regarding her affection are sustained in the consistency of her behaviour. Thus understanding an expressive speech act amounts to the expectation of a certain behaviour of the speaker.

Habermas' general conclusion here is that, in communicative action, only speech acts with which the speaker presents a criticisable validity claim have action-coordinating effects (1984a:I 409–410).

To present a criticisable validity claim means to present a claim which can, if need be, be defended with arguments which might lead to an agreement based on reason. Thus 'simple imperatives', even though they are couched in language, are not a matter of communicative but of linguistically mediated open strategic action.

When the shared understanding a speech act in communicative action aims at is reached, an interpersonal relation is established which is recognised as legitimate (the speaker has endeavoured to perform the *right* speech act in the normative context); some knowledge concerning the *objective world* is shared (the speaker has endeavoured to come up with a true statement) and, finally, some trust has been generated in the credibility of the speaker (the speaker has suggested that s/he has expressed his/her true belief or feeling).

Thus, in communicative action, speech acts serve to renew and repair interpersonal relations, the representation of situations and events and the representation of self. They can also be disputed under each of these three aspects when they are supposed not to be in accordance with the world of legitimately ordered interpersonal relations, the world of external situations and events or the world of subjective experience.

We have said that the illocutionary part of the speech act indicates to which world it specifically refers and we have distinguished between 'constatives' (referring to the objective world), 'regulatives' (referring to the social world) and 'expressives' (referring to the internal world). Though there is in communicative action always a reference to all three worlds at once, this difference in speech acts allows us to specify under which aspect we want to discuss a validity claim.

Let us look once more at the example given above to clarify the point that there is in communicative action, oriented to shared understanding, always a reference to all three worlds. The validity claim of the steward requesting a passenger to put out her cigarette has specific reference to the world of legitimately ordered interpersonal relations or the social world. It also refers, however, to the other worlds distinguished by Habermas, and therefore his claim can be disputed on more than one ground. The passenger can point to facts in the objective world (the warning signs are not on yet, there are no ashtrays etc.), she can dispute the rightness of the relevant regulations or doubt the sincerity of the steward's request (he only wants to get his own back because she has annoyed him at an earlier stage).

Thus Habermas emphasises that each validity claim can be argued against, or rejected as invalid, on more than one ground. To borrow another example from him: when a professor asks a participant in a seminar to bring her a glass of water this request can be rejected on various grounds. The seminar participant can doubt the normative rightness of the request (no, I cannot be treated as a servant) or that conditions in the objective world are appropriate (there are no taps in this building) or the sincerity of the request (you don't want a glass of water, you only want to put me in a rather humiliating position). Thus a hearer can say 'no' under three aspects: 'He or she can say no to the truth of the statement asserted . . . , to the rightness of the utterance in relation to a normative context (or to the rightness of an underlying norm of action itself), and finally to the truthfulness or sincerity of the intention expressed by the speaker' (Habermas, 1982:271–72).

The classification of speech acts referred to above (constative, regulative and expressive) has also enabled Habermas to distinguish between the following three 'pure' types of communicative action: conversation (constituted by constative speech acts), norm-regulated action (here the regulative speech acts have constitutive significance) and dramaturgical action (expressive speech acts predominate) (Habermas, 1984a:I 327–28).

Communicative action rarely consists of only one of these types, but nevertheless this distinction between conversation, norm-regulated action and dramaturgical action is of great importance to Habermas because it enables him to specify in greater detail the various dimensions of the rationality of action. We have to emphasise again that here we are on a basic point. If Habermas had committed himself, like Weber and the early Frankfurters before him, to the recognition, on the level of action, of only one dimension of rationality (that of goalrationality) he would also have been committed to their theory of rationalisation with its exclusively pessimistic conclusions. We have remarked before that central to Habermas' concerns has been the development and defence of a wider concept of rationality which is based on the awareness of the linguistic dimensions of reason and the recognition of collective learning processes, not only in the technological-scientific but also the moral-practical domain.

On the basis of the distinction in pure types of communicative action which Habermas has introduced, the various aspects of the possible rationalisation of action can now be analysed. The dimensions of rationality are, according to Habermas, as follows. *Teleological action,* that is action oriented to a goal, can be judged on its effectiveness. The technical and strategic knowledge involved can be criticised, with regard to its claims to truth, by drawing on the fund of empirical-theoretical knowledge. *Constative speech acts* constituting conversation can also be criticised with regard to their claims to truth. The partners in interaction can switch to the level of *theoretical discourse* in the case of controversy. *Norm-regulated action* embodies moral-practical knowledge and can be queried on the basis of its claim to rightness. This claim can be thematised in practical discourse. *Dramaturgical action* can be criticised as insincere and a form of deception or self-deception. The discourse in which self-deception is dealt with is *therapeutic* in character (Habermas, 1984a:I 333ff).

Habermas' concept of communicative rationality thus refers to these various dimensions of action. He proposes to analyse the process of rationalisation on the basis of this concept rather than to follow Weber in looking selectively at the institutionalisation of goalrational action.

The fact that, unlike Weber, Habermas makes use of a concept of social action, in which the element of achieving shared understanding, rather than that of achieving a result, is made central, also means that his view of *Verstehen,* that is, of the social scientist's achievement of interpretive understanding, is bound to be different from that of Weber.

At first sight it even seems very different. For Habermas 'interpretive understanding' implies judging, thus the very thing we believe Weber was against. The interpreting social scientist, says Habermas, has to give up, in his activity of interpretation, the point of view of the external observer and adopt the performative attitude of the participant in action. He has to take the validity claims of acting agents seriously in order to understand them. This is because the meaning of utterances is dependent on the conditions under which they are valid. These conditions have to be identified, within the context in which the utterances are made, from the point of view of the agents. This amounts to answering the question which reasons agents had to accept, or reject, the validity of utterances. These reasons can only be understood when they are interpreted rationally, that is judged with rationality as a norm.

Weber's view of *Verstehen*, 'interpretive understanding', is less different from this than might at first appear to be the case. In the procedure of *Verstehen* he has outlined, the rationality of action is judged in a process in which the interpreter, through a series of (initially often failing) hypotheses, gradually approaches the point of view of the actual agents. Let us take an example (for the historical accuracy of which we cannot vouch). The strategists who had to interpret German actions in the Battle of Britain tried to 'understand' these by, as Weber said we should do in these cases, constructing 'unreal' rational connections (between the assumed reasons for, the assumed means chosen in, and the factually observed results of action) to find the real connections. Understanding initially broke down when they observed that Goering's airforce ultimately concentrated on destroying London rather than the airstrips in Southern England, though this latter course of action would have seemed to be far more rational from the point of view of what could be presumed to be Germany's main aim in all this, namely to inflict maximum damage on the British war machine, and particularly the RAF. Understanding is, however, not gained by declaring action to be irrational as soon as the first hypothesis fails, but by checking whether it could be found to be rational in a context which is more similar to the one in which the agent himself judged his action. In this particular example: did Hitler's decision to concentrate on London perhaps make sense in a context, a definition of the situation in which domestic political factors (e.g., in this case, the public vow that a thousandfold retribution would be made on London if a single bomb fell on Berlin, which indeed happened at that time) weighed more heavily than his interpreters on the other side of the Channel originally assumed? The point here is that in trying to gain understanding one is pushed further and further in the process of judging the rationality of action from the agent's point of view, that is into what Habermas calls the performative attitude. With the process of *Verstehen* as Weber presents it, this judgment in the performative attitude remains limited to one type of validity claim, namely those specifically referring to the objective world which agents have constructed for themselves. With Habermas this is extended to the interpreter's judgment of all types of validity claim, hence also those referring to norms and values (pertaining to the social world) and the world of inner states and feelings.

'A hearer', said Habermas in answer to a critic who doubted his version of interpretive understanding, 'knows the content of what is said when he knows what reasons (or what sort of reasons) the speaker would give for the validity of his speech act (under appropriate circumstances).' But reasons are of a special nature.

> They can always be expanded into arguments which we then understand only when we recapitulate . . . them in the light of some standards of rationality . . . The interpretative reconstruction of reasons makes it necessary . . . for us to place 'their' standards in relation to 'ours', so that in the case of a contradiction we either revise our preconceptions or relativize 'their' standards of rationality against 'ours', [hence] we *cannot* understand reasons without at least implicitly evaluating them. (Habermas, 1985:204)

And again, 'One can understand reasons only to the extent that one understands why they are or are not sound'.

Habermas' views on these matters have been formulated explicitly also in relation to the debate on rationality in anthropology, in which the central question is whether 'rationality' is culture-bound or whether, on the contrary, it has a universal structure. He takes the latter position but adds the qualification that this holds only if rationality is not identified just with goalrationality but regarded as also having to do with validity claims concerning the social world and the world of inner states and feelings, in other words when that wider concept of rationality is adopted which fits in with a correct analysis of communicative action.

Admittedly, the stance Habermas defends here seems quite alien to the average anthropologist (less so to the historian) who would find it difficult to accept that understanding requires judging. Yet Habermas insists that validity claims cannot be understood without being taken seriously, and that taking them seriously requires that people take a stand towards them.

It is clear then that as far as his view of *Verstehen* is concerned Habermas goes much further than Weber, especially since he seems to expect that the scientific interpreter will not only ask the question whether the agent did or did not follow a certain norm but also raise the allegedly related question whether the norm concerned is right or not. Habermas believes that only by asking this latter question, again from the attitude of a potential participant, the observer can understand the rationally motivating force these norms have for the agents concerned. This point especially has drawn a lot of criticism from his commentators. One point of doubt is whether agents themselves normally ask the question whether a norm referred to in a validity claim, raised in communicative action, is right or not. We will comment at greater length on this in the last chapter.

Here we want to deal with the other obvious problem raised by Habermas' picture of the process of *Verstehen*, namely how the social scientist can retain a certain 'objectivity' if he has to interpret by judging in the performative attitude, that is, by being a participant with participants. Habermas' answer here is that the same communicative rationality which allows access to the object also guarantees the possibility of critical distance and reflection. Claims to truth, normative rightness and sincerity and authenticity involve structures of rationality which have a universal character. The only difference between participant agents and the social scientist here is that the latter might operate under fewer constraints, impeding the switch to a level of discourse which is in principle, though not always in practice, open to agents as well.

Communicative action does not only draw on explicit knowledge. It in fact takes place against the background of an enormous fund of non-explicit, taken-for-granted notions, which have great influence on the interpretation of explicit utterances. Following a phenomenological tradition in philosophy and sociology here, Habermas uses the term 'Lifeworld' to indicate this background. Though this 'Lifeworld' has great influence on the endless range of interpretive activities which constitute social life, we cannot become conscious of it as a whole and sum it up in a series of neat propositions. There is always a horizon behind a horizon. Agents draw on their common Lifeworld to seek shared understanding about something in the objective, social or subjective world. They harmonise their plan of action on the basis of a common definition of the situation, and the 'stock of knowledge' provided by the Lifeworld serves as a resource in this. In using elements of the Lifeworld they also renew and change it.

Normally taken-for-granted notions are just that, taken for granted. One way of becoming conscious of them is for partners in interaction not to share them. Interaction then can consist of a series of 'misunderstandings'. This kind of thing happens frequently in the contact between people belonging to different cultures.

Habermas does not, however, regard the Lifeworld as just a storehouse of frameworks of interpretation. In this view, which in sociology goes back to Schütz and, more recently, Berger and Luckmann, the theory of society, Habermas asserts, has been reduced to a theory of knowledge. For Habermas communicative action, which takes place in the Lifeworld, but also sustains and continues it, is more than just a process of reaching agreement on claims referring to the objective, social and inner world. It is also an activity in which agents 'develop, confirm, and renew their memberships in social groups and their own identities' (Habermas, 1987:II 139).

It is not only in the Schützian tradition that this is not taken sufficiently into account. The Lifeworld concept of some other sociological schools is too narrow as well. In the tradition going back to Durkheim, the theory of society is based on a Lifeworld concept which has been reduced to its aspect of social integration. For George Herbert Mead again, and the sociologists inspired by him, the Lifeworld is mainly a matter of the socialisation of individuals. These sociological representatives of 'symbolic interactionism' see communicative action mainly as the playing, taking over and creation of roles. Culture and society are regarded as a medium for lifelong socialisation processes.

For Habermas communicative action and the Lifeworld involve more than just culture, or social interaction, or socialisation. Communicative action, he says, has the following functions:

> Under the functional aspect of *mutual understanding,* communicative action serves to transmit and renew cultural knowledge; under the aspect of *coordinating action,* it serves social integration and the establishment of solidarity; finally, under the aspect of *socialization,* communicative action serves the formation of personal identities. (Habermas, 1987:II 137)

We see in this passage the basic distinction Habermas makes between three structural components of the Lifeworld: society, culture and personality. We must add here a few remarks to clarify the nature of this distinction. By calling part of the Lifeworld society Habermas does not imply that it coincides with *the whole* of society. If that were the case his distinction between Lifeworld and System, to which we will come back at the end of this chapter, would be meaningless. Habermas defines society in this context as 'the legitimate orders through which participants [in communication] regulate their memberships in social groups and thereby secure solidarity' (1987;II 138).

Culture stands here for the stock of knowledge which provides those who seek shared understanding about something with interpretations. Finally, personality is defined as those 'competences that make a subject capable of speaking and acting, that put him in a position to take part in processes of reaching understanding and thereby to assert his own identity' (1987:II 138).

We should in no way identify the Lifeworld and its elements with the three formal world concepts which have been repeatedly mentioned in the previous pages. The Lifeworld, says Habermas, 'is constitutive for mutual understanding *as such,* whereas the formal world concepts constitute a reference system for that *about which* mutual understanding is possible: speakers and hearers come to an understanding from out of their common Lifeworld about something in the objective, social, or subjective worlds' (1987:II 126).

For Habermas social evolution is, primarily, the process of the rationalisation of the Lifeworld. In this process the Lifeworld's various elements get more and more differentiated. The more these structural components of the Lifeworld are differentiated, the more interaction becomes dependent on rationally motivated shared understanding, 'that is, of consensus formation that rests *in the end* on the authority of the better argument' (1987:II 145).

Habermas believes that the analysis of the rationalisation of the Lifeworld can be systematised under the following points of view. In the first place there is a process of *structural differentiation* here which, as far as the relation between culture and society is concerned, involves the increasing disconnection of institutional systems from world views; which, in the relation between personality and society, involves the coming about of an increasing scope for the creation of interpersonal relations; which, finally, in the relation between culture and personality involves the fact that the renewal of tradition becomes increasingly dependent on the critical and innovative activities of individuals.

The rationalisation of the Lifeworld involves, secondly, a *differentiation between form and content* in each of the three elements of the Lifeworld: culture, society and personality. Habermas sees, on the cultural level, a process in which the core of cultural traditions is transformed into formal elements such as concepts of the world, procedures of argumentation, abstract basic values etc., and is thus increasingly separated from the concrete contents of these traditions.

The separation between form and content is further found, on the level of society, in the fact that the principles which have to do with the existence of a legal order and morality also become increasingly abstract and formal and are related less and less to concrete contents.

Finally, on the level of the personality, one sees the separation between form and content manifested in the fact that cognitive structures are increasingly disjoined from the concrete contents of cultural knowledge. As one commentator puts it: the individual 'develops competences that may be used in a variety of different settings. Development of the "formal-operational" skill of quantitative reasoning, for instance, serves the bank teller, the actuary, the engineer, and the marketing director, albeit in certain occupationally specific ways' (Baxter, 1987:51).

A third aspect of the rationalisation of the Lifeworld is the *increasing, functional specification of processes of the reproduction of culture, society and personality.* Habermas speaks in this context of the 'increasing reflexivity' of symbolic reproduction, a term with which he refers to the increased scope for criticism, reflection on established practices and concomitant changes in a rationalising Lifeworld. In terms of the differentiation between culture, society and personality one can think here of the way in which, for the pursuit of the sciences, humanities and arts, specific institutions and forms of discourse are developed (culture). One can think here of the coming about of specific institutions in the political sphere which provide the basis for 'discursive formation of the will' in political matters (society). One can, finally, think here of specific institutions for the education of the young and the reflection on education as a specialised task in the form of pedagogy (personality) (Habermas, 1987:II 146-47).

Thus, in this process of rationalisation, the world views implicit in the Lifeworld are made more and more explicit. They differentiate and get 'split up' and embodied in various realms of knowledge and institutions. Why does this clarifying process, in which the implicit becomes more and more explicitly formulated and criticisable, and the scope for rational rather than empirical motivation initially increases, lead to the paradoxical consequences which Weber indicated as 'loss of meaning' and 'loss of freedom'? Not, for Habermas, as Weber and those who are inspired by him have it, because of the increasing and undue prominence of goalrationality. Weber, says Habermas, did not get the rationalisation process properly in view, not only because his concept of action was inadequate but also, and mainly, because he merely looked at society from the perspective of the participant actor. That perspective is too one-sided for Habermas. We have already seen that he argues that we should look at society both on the level of action and on that of the system. Society does not only consist of the communicatively structured Lifeworld but also of the System. Here Habermas makes a distinction between two forms of integration of society: *social integration,* which takes place via the action orientations of participant agents, and *system integration,* which is a matter of the functional intertwining of action consequences. There is no case for either looking exclusively at the former, as action theorists are inclined to do, or the latter, which systems theorists have a tendency to do. Society should be conceived of as both System *and* Lifeworld, says Habermas. This has, of course, its consequences for the study of rationalisation.

In the evolutionary process which we indicated with the term . rationalisation, the differentiation of the Lifeworld starts to impose such heavy demands on the interpretive capacities of actors that whole areas of action, mainly in the field of economics and government administration, 'drop out of language' as it were and find functional interaction in the System. Thus the study of rationalisation analyses this process, and its interrelations, in both Lifeworld and System. Let us have a closer look at Habermas' account of this and his discussion of the concept of System and systemic integration.

4
Rationalisation and the System

If modern society was mainly held together by communicative action it would be far more transparent than it actually is, and it would not befall human beings, as it does befall them now, that they are repeatedly confronted with situations in which nobody recognises what he or she wants.

It is also on the basis of this common experience that we can understand Habermas' distinction between two forms of integration of society, namely social integration, which comes about through communicative action, and system or functional integration which has to do with the intertwining of the consequences of action. It is not the least aspect of Habermas' contribution to sociology that he has not dealt with analysis in terms of action and in terms of structure or system as an 'either . . . or' but as an 'and . . . and'. Society has to be analysed on both levels. From the *objectivating attitude,* which is characteristic for system-theoretical analyses, one can gain access to functional relations (which for the social agents themselves remain largely out of sight) but not to the distinctive nature of communicative processes. This can, according to Habermas, only be perceived from the perspective of the participant in a certain Lifeworld, that is from a *performative attitude.* In fact, it is Habermas' conviction that one can only by this two-pronged approach explain phenomena which Marx, Weber and Durkheim signalled under different names (alienation, the 'iron cage', anomie) but did not adequately analyse. These phenomena can, according to Habermas, only be explained from the mutual relations between System and Lifeworld, which makes the clear conceptual distinction of these different orders of integration a necessity. The decisive element in the explanation of these phenomena is the account of social evolution as a process of the coming

39

about of the System on the basis of the rationalisation of the Lifeworld, the increasing complexity of the System and rationality of the Lifeworld and the disjunction between these two, and finally, the invasion of core Lifeworld areas by systemic mechanisms. This latter phenomenon Habermas calls the 'colonisation of the Lifeworld'.

Here we will first look at Habermas' account of the historical stages of this process of rationalisation and then, via a discussion of one of its most important aspects, namely the rationalisation of law, analyse it on a higher level of abstraction (cf. Habermas, 1987:II 156ff).

Societies have the task of symbolic *and* material reproduction, of which the latter, as we have seen, has to do with the preservation of bodies through the production and distribution of goods and services. In *archaic society,* says Habermas, the performance of these tasks is still intertwined and embedded in the kinship system. Part of the circulation of economic goods remains dependent on marriage relations. In the exchange of women social and system integration coincide. The mutual identity of systemic and social integration is, in this kind of *egalitarian tribal society,* also based on mythical world views which provide a charter for social structure as a whole as well as for daily interaction.

The exchange creates a network of social relations along which the exchange of other goods and services takes place. The ritual exchange of valuable objects can become a functional equivalent of the exchange of women. This latter exchange can also bring about a *society with segmentary differentiation.* Subgroups can come about through similar social units being joined to bigger units of the same structure. With this vertical layering of unilinear descent groups differences in power originate which can be used for organisational purposes. Such organisational means can find application because of the division of labour, which gradually gains a foothold under the impetus of the intuitive endeavour to put the least possible effort in the general task of the species to survive through an exchange with nature. This task is conducive to the origination of subsystems of goalrational action which are structured via exchange and power mechanisms, that is systemic mechanisms which are at this stage not yet separated from the institutions which create social integration. In this sense these *hierarchical tribal societies,* as Habermas calls them, are not yet basically different from the egalitarian ones.

This changes when political authority comes about, which does not get its prestige from descent groups but rather from the disposal over the means of judicial sanction. Power mechanisms are disconnected from the kinship structure and become the core for the crystallisation of a new institution, namely the state. At this stage of development the cultural support, through mythical world views, for a situation in which systemic and social integration coincide is eroded in a process which Habermas calls the 'linguistification of the sacred'. This implies a shift in the burden of social integration from a religiously anchored consensus to linguistic processes of consensus formation. Habermas calls this type of society *politically stratified class society.*

Within the framework of this, goods markets can originate which are coordinated through the medium of money. When, ultimately, the economy splits off from the political order, money can have a structurating effect on the whole of society. The economic subsystem can induce reorganisations of the state. Then the fourth type of society, distinguished in this context by Habermas, comes about: *economically constituted class society.*

Thus there are, according to this account, four evolutionary levels of system differentiation, namely segmentary differentiation, stratification, the state, and the steering media of power and money, which prevail, respectively, in egalitarian tribal society, hierarchical tribal society, politically stratified class society and economically constituted class society.

Throughout this course of social evolution, System differentiation and differentiation within the Lifeworld remain tied up with each other in the sense that only new institutional complexes in the Lifeworld provide 'anchorage' for new systemic mechanisms. In egalitarian tribal societies this anchorage is provided by sex and generation roles; in hierarchical tribal societies by status descent groups; in politically stratified class societies by political office, and in economically constituted class societies by bourgeois civil law. The coming about of these new institutional complexes in the Lifeworld, in which the newly developing systemic mechanisms have to be anchored, is a matter of the institutionalisation of increasingly abstract forms of action oriented to shared understanding. This is one aspect of the rationalisation of the Lifeworld.

We can understand institutional complexes which at each stage provide 'anchorage' in the Lifeworld for differentiation within the System as the 'basis' of society. Though the stimulus for the differentiation of the social system comes in the first place from the realm of material production, it is clear from what has been said above that this 'basis' is not to be *identified* with the economic structure of society. The distinction between basis and super-structure can be given an evolutionary connotation. It is at each stage within the parameters set by the 'basis' that systemic problems come about which must be solved on a higher level of system differentiation.

At the stage of social evolution where we can speak of economic-ally constituted class societies, some of the functions relevant for society are depoliticised and delegated to subsystems separate from the state. The depoliticisation of the economic subsystem is made possible by the new medium of money, which takes this subsystem out of a normative context. The exchange with the non-economic environment, the state and private households, also takes place via money. Through its need for resources the state becomes dependent on the economic subsystem. Political power acquires the structure of a medium of taxation and is assimilated to money. Capitalistic enterprise and the modern state administration are autonomous organisations in the sense that people belong to them on the basis of specific expectations about their behaviour. Thus the organisations are independent from communicatively structured Lifeworld con-texts and concrete value orientations. This can be made clear by taking an example from modern organisations, for instance a bank. The main goal of this organisation is to make profit, yet those who work there might be largely indifferent to that goal. They go to their place of work to make money for their family, to pass the day in the least unpleasant way possible, to see colleagues etc., yet withal much of their behaviour fits into the pattern of activities which lead to the bank's profit. Habermas quotes Luckmann on this point: '... in most of the areas of everyday life important for maintaining a society, the objective meaning of an action no longer coincides as a matter of course with the subjective sense of acting' (Luckmann, quoted in Habermas, 1987:II 311).

This line of analysis does not only apply when the subjective meaning of the individual's action, within the context of his or her individual life, is compared with its objective meaning within the context of the organisation. One can analyse the discrepancy which often exists between the manifest and the latent functions of an organisation along similar lines. A well-known example was pro-vided in the classic work of Thomas and Znaniecki on the Polish peasant in Europe and America. These authors pointed out that the Polish peasant cooperative institutions had a social function which was in no way limited to their manifest purpose. They constituted, in fact, an 'intermediary link between the peasant primary group and the secondary national system' and thus contributed to the overall functional integration of society, even though this contribution had not been planned (cf. Merton, 1957:62).

The 'System' is thus encountered, from the inner perspective of the Lifeworld, as something in the objective world, which is no longer accessible for the 'pre-understanding' of communicative everyday praxis. Its analysis requires special sciences, the social sciences, which originate around the eighteenth century.

Habermas' notion that new levels of System differentiation require institutional anchorage in the Lifeworld can be most fittingly illustrated by his views on the development of law and morality. Characteristic of this development is their differentiation and separation from each other. Morality gets deinstitutionalised and limited to a place in the personality system where it functions as an internal control on behaviour. Law becomes an externally imposed power, dependent on abstract obedience and disjoined from the moral motivation of those subject to it. This development cannot take place as long as the whole of social organisation remains embedded within the kinship system. The validity of norms then remains rooted in the ritual actions of the community and is not supported by external sanctions monopolised by a judicial overlord. This is all different in state societies. Here political authority is based on the legitimate disposal over sanctions. Judicial power is not based on birth but on the legitimacy of a legal order which structurally requires an office from which this order is protected and kept up. Around this office political authority can crystallise and a political order come about which at first envelopes a society in which most transactions are still based on traditional morality. This changes, says Habermas, when the economy becomes, through the medium of money, a neutralised action system. Transactions then become morally neutral and oriented towards results. Law is transformed into a means of organisation to be used in a goalrational way. A disjunction appears, in the course of legal development, between morality and formal law. This is concomitant with the disjunction between social and systemic integration.

Habermas deems it typical for modern law that the 'roads to legitimacy' have lengthened in the sense that the legality of single decisions is guaranteed by correct procedure and that only the legal system *as a whole* needs to be anchored in institutions which provide legitimacy, such as constitutional law and the principle of democratic rule. He refers here to influence and prestige as the basis for mechanisms which provide relief from the burden of reaching shared understanding. Influence and prestige induce a willingness to follow and accept consensus in a shortcut through the whole intricate tangle of validity claims. In the course of evolution this willingness comes to be induced by the legal authority of the state, rather than influential persons and is, finally, transformed into an abstract obedience to the law. In morally neutralised action systems, such as the economy, single actions are justified by the correctness of procedures prescribed by a body of law which is only legitimated as a whole.

Let us have a closer look at the coming about of the relief mechanisms for communicative action within the context of the overall process of rationalisation. We saw, in the previous chapter, that Habermas rejects, at one and the same time, a too narrow definition of both Lifeworld and communicative action, by stressing that communicative action serves the transmission and renewal of cultural knowledge, the continuation of stable institutions ('society') and the socialisation of accountable persons. In this way communicative action serves the reproduction of the symbolic structures of the Lifeworld, which should be distinguished, as we saw, from the replenishment of its material substratum. The more the differentiation of the Lifeworld into culture, society and personality progresses, the more interaction becomes dependent on rationally motivated shared understanding, which is ultimately based on 'the authority of the better argument'.

Rationalisation thus implies, according to Habermas, an enhanced criticisability of the cultural tradition over its whole range. Greater and greater areas of what was merely taken for granted are transformed into cultural knowledge, and used for the attainment of shared definitions of the situation in communicative action. But with this transformation into knowledge, the 'merely taken for granted' also becomes exposed to critical tests. Where the formal world concepts have not yet been clearly differentiated, world views are protected against 'dissonant experiences'. With increasing rationalisation this protection disappears. The reproduction of the Lifeworld becomes more and more a matter of the conscious achievements of the agents themselves. The renewal of traditions thus gets more and more dependent on the critical and innovative capacities of individuals. These activities express the potential for rationality inherent in communicative action.

We indicated above that one aspect of social evolution has to do with the increasing disjunction of System and Lifeworld. Let us have a closer look at the phenomena which are at the basis of this. The increasing dependence of the reproduction of the symbolic structure of the Lifeworld on the interpretive capacities of agents, which is entailed by rationalisation, creates difficulties. The greater this dependence the greater the possibility for misunderstandings and a breakdown of interaction. When the implicit definition of the situation given by ego can be confirmed, modified, partly suspended or made questionable in the exchange between ego and alter, reaching consensus as a basis for the coordination of action is no longer a straightforward matter. However, we saw that these difficulties are partly compensated for by one specific aspect of rationalisation, namely the 'universalisation', of law and morality, which entails the capacity to recognise similar cases as similar and to deal with them in similar ways. In the sphere of morality, which belongs to the social world, this leads to mental structures which prepare the ground for the creation of codified law. The distinction between abstract norms and principles on the one hand, and concrete values and forms of life on the other, becomes continuously clearer. This is important for the coming about, and splitting off from the Lifeworld, of subsystems of goalrational action, such as the government and the market, which can only operate properly on the basis of codified law. Let us look at this in detail.

Habermas reasons here as follows. With the 'linguistification of the sacred' social integration becomes more and more a matter of consensus formation via language. But the clearer this type of coordination of action, via shared understanding, becomes, the clearer also its opposite, strategic and instrumental action, which are oriented to results rather than shared understanding. One of the paradoxes of rationalisation is that the more the 'primeval consensus' in the sphere of the sacred disappears into the background, the more the coordination of action takes place via language, the greater also the necessity for non-linguistic steering media of action such as money and power which induce an empirical rather than, as language does, a rational motivation of action. Why do these non-linguistic steering media become more necessary? As we saw above, the coordination of action via language has its own difficulties. Rationalisation means that greater and greater areas of the Lifeworld are lifted out of the 'pre-understanding' inherent in the religiously anchored consensus and become criticisable. With it the interpretive tasks which are posed by communicative action become increasingly more complex and difficult. The possibilities of misunderstanding and disagreement, the input required to come to agreement, make coordination via language rather too circuitous and troublesome for many affairs of daily life. There is thus a pressure for the formation of *relief mechanisms* in either of two directions: mechanisms which *'condense'* shared understanding, reached via linguistic means, or *replace* it (Habermas, 1987:II 181).

These mechanisms are, in the most general terms, based on such ubiquitous social phenomena as influence and prestige. The more influence and prestige ego has, the more alter is willing to accept his/her claims without further ado. If influence and prestige are based on ego's supposed 'knowledge' in the widest sense (cognitive as well as moral practical knowledge) the motivation of alter, in the ready acceptance of ego's claims, is rational. If influence and prestige are, however, based on other supposed qualities, which make alter believe in ego's capacity to dole out rewards and punishments, alter's motivation to accept ego's claims is 'empirical'.

Habermas asserts that new steering media, functioning as relief mechanisms for communicative action via purely linguistic means, come about when influence and prestige are generalised. These new steering media are, as said above, either based on the 'condensation' of shared understanding, via linguistic means, or on its replacement.

The term 'condensation' stands here for the hierarchisation of validity claims, which is made possible by value generalisation. A clear example is the greater weight which is, in due course, given to the words of the man or woman with a generally recognised professional reputation, as compared to the claims of one who does not have this reputation. Another form of the hierarchisation of validity claims is made possible by what Parsons called the value commitments of group members. This provides the basis for moral leadership.

The generalisation of prestige and influence is dependent on, first, the differentiation of cultural value spheres entailed by value generalisation. A scientific reputation, for instance, can only be established when the cognitive sphere has been differentiated, moral leadership when the moral-practical sphere has become clearly separate. Both kinds of influence also require for their generalisation the coming about of a public sphere, which depends

on new communication technologies (printing press, electronic
media etc.).

Relief mechanisms for communicative action which *replace*
linguistic understanding have a different character. Such media as
money and power *empirically* (rather than rationally) motivate
partners in interaction. They *replace* linguistic communication.
Money helps to reduce complexity in everyday situations which
have become too involved to be dealt with in a mere exchange of
validity claims. As Simmel points out in his *Philosophy of Money,*

> A price in money . . . creates unity; its parts, thanks to the total lack of
> differentiation between them, constitute such a complete unity as
> hardly exists anywhere else in a practical area. People can even say of
> such a valuable and many-sided object, as for instance a manorial
> estate, that it is worth half a million marks. This sum then
> comprehends its value in a unifying concept, on however many
> considerations and presuppositions this value is based. (Simmel,
> 1930:187)

The new steering media allow the coming about of subsystems
which become *independent* of the Lifeworld. They provide the basis
for more and more complicated networks of interaction, in which
individual actors can no longer have an overview of, nor feel
individual responsibility for, events. These new steering mechanisms become to a high degree independent from the Lifeworld,
though they are dependent for their operation on codified law
which, in its turn, is only made possible by the universalisation
entailed by the rationalisation of the Lifeworld. The new forms of
integration, which operate via these steering media, the state and
the market, have 'dropped out of language' as it were. Integration
does not take place here through the process of reaching shared
understanding, in an exchange of more or less explicit, more or less
criticisable validity claims, but 'behind the backs of actors'. Action
coordination (which should be distinguished from the *integration* of
the System as such) comes about, in the first instance, through ego
motivating alter empirically, rather than rationally (via validity
claims), to perform certain actions: in the market through offering a
certain sum of money and, in the sphere of the government, through
the implicit or explicit threat with sanctions. Action consequences
are intertwined in the System on a level which is not directly
accessible to everyday social 'pre-understanding'. Agents relate to
such action systems as they would to a piece of nature.

For instance, we tend to regard changes in the stock market, though these are ultimately the outcome of human actions, as rather similar to changes in the weather, and long-term predictions about the real estate market have about the same credibility as long-term weather predictions. The System, containing these forms of integration, splits off from the Lifeworld, though it depended for its development on the rationalisation of this in the first place. This coming about of the market depends, as we saw above, on the legal development which led among other things to the protection of property and that of contracts by law. The origination of institutionalised government is based on specific forms of the belief in legitimacy. The actual functioning of the steering media money and power is, however, *not* dependent on the Lifeworld processes of reaching shared understanding via language. In this sense the System is norm-free and 'delinguistified' even though, of course, we still do find the use of language here for purposes of communication, rather than for the coordination of action via the exchange of validity claims.

There is thus a disjunction of systemic integration, via the new steering media money and power, and social integration in the Lifeworld. These new systemic structures ultimately become so independent that they can be no longer controlled from the Lifeworld.

It is this coming about of the System and its uncoupling from the Lifeworld which requires us to expose and abandon a few fictions found not only in the 'inner perspective' of actors but also inherent in a one-sidedly 'culturalistic' interpretive sociology.

The first of these fictions concerns the *supposed autonomy of agents,* the idea of social process as based on the will and consciousness of the adult members of society; the second has to do with the *supposed autonomy of culture.* The Lifeworld, says Habermas, constitutes from the perspective of actors a horizon they cannot go beyond. From this perspective it does not even make sense to ask whether culture is empirically dependent on something else. The last fiction concerns the *perspicuity of action.* Agents believe that, in principle, they can seek shared understanding about everything. From this perspective a pseudo-consensus, which is really based on convictions forged by power, simply cannot exist.

Fictions like these are entertained by a sociology which identifies Lifeworld and society, and assumes that the integration of the latter is based *entirely* on action oriented to shared understanding. It suffers from the hermeneutic idealism, says Habermas, which we find in the phenomenological, linguistic and ethnomethodological varieties of an interpretive sociology, which often does not go beyond 'reformulations of a more or less trivial everyday knowledge' (Habermas, 1987:II 148).

This kind of 'hermeneutic idealism' would be justified if the necessary reproduction of the Lifeworld only concerned its symbolical structure. However, its material structure also has to be reproduced and it is exactly there that we see the functioning of the newly developing steering media such as money and power.

These media have by their nature nothing to do with the symbolic structure of the Lifeworld, which can only be reproduced in action oriented to shared understanding. They provide, as we saw, relief mechanisms as far as the material reproduction of society is concerned. The functional integration of the Sytem is based on the intertwining of the non-intended consequences of action. This is quite clear as far as the market is concerned: the functioning of the market is not based on anybody's or any group's particular design but rather on the interlocking consequences of countless individual actions. The System can thus not be understood from the inner perspective of the participant but should be analysed from the outside perspective of the observer. Thus a fully adequate theory of society requires a combination of action theory and system theory. The integration of society can, as we saw, be looked at from two different points of view. *Social integration* is part of the symbolic reproduction of society and is dependent on cultural traditions and processes of socialisation. *Functional integration* is, however, identical with a material reproduction of the Lifeworld, and can also be conceived of as maintenance of the System. The analysis of these different forms of integration requires a different methodological approach and conceptual apparatus. 'The latest functions of action call for the concept of a systemic interdependency that goes beyond the communicative intermeshing of action orientations' (Habermas, 1987:II 233). The overall integration of society requires that the value orientations on which symbolic reproduction is based do conform to the functional demands of System reproduction. If this is not the case social cohesion is only preserved if the relevant functions remain latent, that is, if actors remain unaware of them. This is only possible if communication is systematically limited and distorted. The false consciousness which results from this is manifested on the collective level as ideology, and/or on the individual level as self-deception. When Habermas speaks of the 'colonisation of the Lifeworld' he has in mind, however, a far more serious form of the interference by functional integration with social integration. Ultimately it is these very relief mechanisms of money and power which turn against the Lifeworld in a process which Habermas has compared to the penetration of colonial overlords in a tribal society. Let us have a closer look at his account of this process.

5

The 'colonisation of the Lifeworld'

It is in his views on what he calls the 'colonisation of the Lifeworld' that Habermas' position as not merely an academic philosopher and sociologist but as a critical theorist is most clearly expressed.

We saw above that, according to him, there are in Western history two processes of rationalisation, that of the System and that of the Lifeworld, which gradually diverge in the transition to modernity. These two processes of rationalisation are interconnected. The rationalisation of the System is initially dependent on that of the Lifeworld but has, at the stage of late capitalism, in a process which Habermas calls 'colonisation', turned back on the Lifeworld in a destructive fashion.

Before we consider Habermas' account of these matters we should look again at a point we have referred to at various stages above, namely that he does not present the 'colonisation of the Lifeworld' as the inevitable, or the only, outcome of rationalisation. He does not regard it to be the only outcome because he recognises more than one dimension to the rationalisation process. He does not accept it as inevitable because he makes a careful distinction between the logic and the dynamics of development. This distinction should be clearly understood because it plays a fundamental part in his argument. The logic of development has to do with learning processes, which can be 'internally reconstructed' as problem solutions by looking at them from the perspective of participants. The mental development which is set going by the attempt to solve a specific and universal problem in religious world views (we will indicate in the chapters on Weber which problem this is) leads to the coming about of the capacity to distinguish clearly between the various formal world concepts and the different validity claims regarding these realms; it also leads to the ability to take a critical distance towards these claims or, as Habermas puts in, to take 'yes' or 'no' positions towards them.

This learning process, this advance in competence, coincides with the differentiation in world views. The more this differentiation process has taken place, the stronger the need for people to coordinate their action on the basis of an agreed definition of the situation reached via validity claims, and the greater also the possibility for criticism. A mythical world view, in which the various world perspectives are still inextricably intertwined, is, as we saw, more or less immunised against criticism.

Habermas seeks support and inspiration for his views on the logic of development in the ideas of the Swiss psychologist Piaget. Piaget's theories, on which we will touch briefly here, concern the intellectual and moral development of children. One concept of Piaget which is particularly important to Habermas is that of 'decentration'. Piaget uses this to refer to the process in which children learn to distinguish between themselves and the external reality of their environment. In this learning process the child acquires the competence to 'decenter' the originally pivotal place which it gives to itself in its environment. It learns to differentiate and cope with the external world, the social world and the world of 'inner subjectivity'—we recognise Habermas' formal world concepts.

Habermas uses Piaget's term 'decentration' to indicate the extent to which the acceptance or rejection of validity claims is influenced by frameworks of interpretation stored in the Lifeworld. The more decentration has taken place the less is this influence, because large areas of the Lifeworld have, as we saw, been lifted from 'pre-understanding' and become criticisable. Quite apart from this specific concept of 'decentration', Habermas owes to Piaget the very idea of a 'logic of development'. Whereas in the 'genetic structuralism' of Piaget this stands for the development of the structures of individual consciousness, Habermas applies it to the species as such. Piaget's structures of consciousness become, in Habermas' account of the evolution of the species, 'structures of world views'. The transition from one world view to another is a matter of changes in fundamental categorial concepts. With the transition from one such system of concepts to another the interpretations of an earlier epoch lose, as it were, their entire foundation. They are 'categorically devalued'. We can think here, for instance, as far as the 'objective world' is concerned, of the 'Copernican revolution' in ideas on cosmology; an obvious example in relation to the 'social world' is the disappearance of the knightly ideal from post-medieval Europe. Habermas hypothesises that such transitions are connected with transitions to new levels of learning. The conditions for learning change in the dimensions of "objectivating thought, moral-practical insight, and the aesthetic-expressive capacity' (Habermas, 1984:I 687). Thus changes in world views are linked up to the species' increasing capacity to differentiate between, and make use of, the three formal world concepts.

Whether the collective learning process, which coincides with the rationalisation of the Lifeworld, actually takes place is a matter not of the logic but of the dynamics of development, that is to say of empirical, contingent factors which can only be understood from the outside. Here too one can think of the comparison with the development of children. Whether a child's capacity for speech, for instance, is actually developed is a matter of contingent factors, as we have learned from the history of Kaspar Hauser and many similar cases. This distinction between the logic and dynamics of development is of great importance to Habermas, because it enables him to argue, against Weber's view of rationalisation for instance, that such development as has actually taken place was not the only possible one, but a matter of historically contingent factors which could just as well have been otherwise. Hence Habermas can regard the 'colonisation of the Lifeworld' as not of necessity inherent in historical development (a view to which Weber and the early Frankfurters tended) but as a pathological development against which resistance is possible. Rationalisation might, instead of this one-sided form, have involved the 'balanced' development of the cognitive as well as the expressive and normative domain, which could have allowed for the normative control of the new subsystems which have money and power as their steering media.

The analysis of the 'colonisation of the Lifeworld' is central to Habermas' theory of communicative action. In an interview he said (in Giddens' recapitulation of his words) that his 'real motive' in writing the book was to clarify how 'the critique of reification', of rationalisation, could be reformulated to offer a theoretical explanation for the decay of the 'welfare state compromise' on the one hand, and the critical potential—embodied in new movements— on the other, 'without discarding the project of modernity or relapsing into post or anti-modernism' (Giddens, 1982: 319).

Habermas speaks of a critique of 'reification' and we should keep in mind here that, in his vocabulary, reification and rationalisation are not identical. The term reification refers to the process in which the rational foundations of communicative action in the Lifeworld are, ultimately, undermined by the 'functional conditions of system reproduction' in modern societies. Economy and state penetrate, via money and power, into the Lifeworld and destroy communicative processes in areas where these remain necessary, namely those of cultural reproduction, social integration and socialisation.

Let us look at some of the concrete phenomena Habermas has in mind here, for instance education. This is not the place to go into historical detail, but few people will dispute the general proposition that universities in the Western world were, originally, forms of cooperation between masters and students. The rationale for that cooperation was, beyond immediate personal interests (which, of course, were also involved) to be found in ideals of learning which were either based on direct religious inspiration or, by contrast, on the emancipatory ambitions of a secular 'intelligentsia'.

In the modern era education, and this is especially the case in higher education, has become increasingly subject to the imperatives emanating from the economic-administrative system. Higher education has to provide the market with trained manpower. Accordingly, in an economic situation in which resources become increasingly scarce, these are allocated in the first place to academic activities of which the 'usefulness' can be demonstrated in macro-economic terms. This means, especially in countries where governments can directly interfere in the decisions of academic institutions, less money and attention for what the Germans call the 'orchid' subjects: that is, subject areas in which the often delicate and exotic flower of learning is tended for its own sake. In our own subject, sociology, it means greater attention for subdisciplines with a direct vocational use rather than for sociology as a general historical-critical enterprise.

Allocation of money on the basis of economic imperatives entails, as a concomitant phenomenon, the direct administrative interference of the government in processes of decision-making which were until then based on the often informal consultative processes of those directly involved. This holds for all areas of education. One aspect of this form of 'colonisation' is the juridification of hitherto informal relations. This is all the more intriguing because the interference by the state here often takes the form of the protection of the involved parties, or one of the parties, against each other. Habermas is referring here specifically to phenomena in West Germany where, as he puts it, the legal protection of students and parents against pedagogical measures (such as test results) and disciplinary measures has been bought at the price of a juridification and bureaucratisation which are interfering deeply in teaching and learning processes.

We will touch, without going into details, on a few more examples of the 'colonisation of the Lifeworld'. Habermas mentions developments in family law and its administration. Juridification means here too, in the first place, the extension of constitutional principles: the protection of the basic rights of the child against his/her parents, the basic rights of the wife against the husband. But here too this implies the opening up of action areas, which were originally not formally organised, for bureaucratic interference and their subsumption under judicial control. Areas of the Lifeworld which are dependent on shared understanding as mechanisms of action coordination are formalised in a way which evokes 'pathological' reactions (particularly in Australia we have seen some telling examples of this). People who have been relating in a communicatively structured realm of action now confront each other as legal subjects in an objectivating disposition. This 'emancipation' of the members of the family in relation to each other is paid for with an increased dependency on the state. Family conflicts are 'solved' by resorting to formal criteria which can, by their nature, not do justice to the specifics of each case. Parental care is 'replaced' by bureaucratic measures which, under the pressure of economic imperatives, often take a totally impersonal administrative form. Arrangements in the area of child maintenance provide a case in point.

We saw above that Habermas uses for all this the telling term 'juridification'. With this he indicates the general tendency in modern society to the expansion and greater refinement of codified law. He makes a distinction here between the development of law as a medium which, functioning in relation to the steering media money and power, is constitutive of formally organised realms of action and the development of legal institutions. These latter forms of law have no constitutive function. They merely regulate already existing communicatively structured realms of action. In the 'colonisation of the Lifeworld' law is, however, also used as a medium in areas which are dependent on communicative action. Central regions of cultural reproduction, social integration and socialisation are then drawn into the dynamics of economic growth and juridified. Habermas is thinking here especially of social legislation, besides such areas of law as we have already referred to above, namely family law and the legislation pertaining to education (1987:II 368–73).

He distinguishes four distinct historical stages in the process of juridification which, though the continuous growth in codified law is probably mainly a matter of its increased use as a medium, are also characterised by the coming about of new legal institutions. The first stage was that of the *bourgeois state* which developed in Western Europe during the time of absolutism. The second was that of the *constitutional state*, for instance the German monarchy during the nineteenth century. The *democratic constitutional state*, originating in Western Europe and North America in the wake of the French Revolution, constituted the third stage. Finally, in the fourth stage, the *social democratic constitutional state* was brought about through the organised struggle of the European labour movement.

If this historical development is indicated in terms of Habermas' theoretical system it looks as follows: with the coming about of the bourgeois state a political order was created in which formally free and equal legal persons were free to enter into contracts and to act instrumentally within the limits defined by law. Codified law guaranteed the calculability of all action which was covered by it.

In the constitutional state, which came into being in the second major stage of juridification, the citizens were also given clearly specified rights vis-à-vis the government, though they could not yet influence the government's action directly. The freedom acquired during the first stage, that of the coming about of the bourgeois state, had a far more ambiguous character, because freedom was then also the freedom of capital to buy labour power in a process leading to the proletarisation of the labourer.

The modern state and its medium power found, subsequently, further 'anchorage' in an institutionalised Lifeworld, when the creation of law was tied up to parliamentary procedures and public debate. Citizens acquired, with this coming about of the democratic constitutional state, the right of political participation. The juridification of the process of legitimation found expression in general and equal voting rights as well as freedom of organisation for political associations and parties. Juridification of legitimation did not do away with the dependency of power on the Lifeworld. Ultimately it was only a structurally differentiated Lifeworld which remained the source of legitimation for the modern state.

Thus during the second and third stages of juridification we see the gradual growth of the unambiguous protection of the freedom of the citizen against the government, and with it the protection of the

Lifeworld. What now is the fate of the Lifeworld during the fourth and final stage of juridification, that of the coming about of the social democratic constitutional state? Does juridification imply the protection of freedom here? On the one hand it seems that the Lifeworld is indeed being protected against the unbridled expansion and dynamics of the economic system via the legal regulation of the exchange between capital and labour, involving specifics of working hours, dismissal procedures, unionism, social insurance etc. On the other hand this same legal regulation implies the 'constitutionalisation' of the power relation implicit in the class structure. The costs of this constitutionalisation are, for the Lifeworld, that areas of life which can only be integrated via communicative action are now being formally organised. Concrete situations, which fit into an individual life story, must be forcibly put into abstract terms so that they can be 'administratively digested'. The bureaucracy will have to work selectively here because 'undigestible' cases will have to be left aside. Also, the inadequacy of monetary 'solutions' for problems which often cannot be redefined in terms of consumption is compensated for by the therapeutic help of social services. These put their clients into a relation of dependency.

Thus law can be the medium for the monetarisation and bureaucratisation of core areas of the Lifeworld. These are split off from action coordination via shared understanding and reintegrated via the media of money and power. Parts of law can become a means of organisation for the System. Legitimation is then merely a matter of correct procedure and a material justification of the law's implementation appears, from the perspective of the Lifeworld, impossible or even meaningless. Large tracts of commercial and administrative law can serve in this way. This is why Habermas can see formal organisation as a criterion for the demarcation of Lifeworld and System. 'I call "formally organized" all social relations located in media-steered subsystems, so far as these relations are *first generated by positive law*' (1987:II 309). Juridification creates possibilities for a strategic treatment of norms and leads to the 'drying up' of processes of spontaneous creation of opinion and will. Other parts of law, especially constitutional law and criminal law, remain tied up to the Lifeworld because they need material justification. Legitimation through correct procedure is impossible here.

The 'pacification' policy of the social democratic welfare state must use law as a medium. In that form it is applied to realms of action which are systemically integrated, though it extends to areas which are embedded in informal Lifeworld contexts.

Juridification is one aspect of the way in which formally organised realms of action, which come about with the differentiation and development of the steering media of money and power, become indifferent towards the various aspects of the Lifeworld, such as culture, personality and society. As far as the personality is concerned, organisations make themselves independent from the concrete dispositions and particular goals—in general from the personal background—of their members. We have already given an example of this in the previous chapter when we referred to the fact that in a modern business organisation (we spoke in our particular example of a bank) personnel can be largely indifferent to the main organisational goal. The development which led to phenomena such as this started with the separation between the capitalistic enterprise and the household of the entrepreneur. Organisations also make themselves independent from the cultural tradition and only use cultural elements for purposes of self-legitimation. Finally, a historically important example of their neutralisation against society is the separation between the secularised state and the church.

The rationalisation of the Lifeworld which led to the split-up between Lifeworld and System, and ultimately the 'colonisation' of the former by the latter, was a process of differentiation. Capitalism and the modern state developed, via the media of money and power, from the Lifeworld's societal components, that is its system of institutions. After this development the Lifeworld is limited to the socially integrated, complementary private and public sphere. The institutional core of the former is the nuclear family, which is freed from economic tasks and specialised in the task of socialisation. The institutional core of the public sphere is to be found in the 'culture industry', press and, later, mass media.

The exchange relations between System and Lifeworld are then, from the perspective of the former, as follows. The economic system exchanges wages against labour power and goods and services against consumer demands. The system of public administration exchanges organisational achievements against taxes and political decisions against mass loyalty. Thus we see the monetarisation of labour power and the bureaucratisation of state activity.

Complementary Lifeworld roles which crystallise around these exchange relations are those of employee and consumer (the economic system) and client and citizen (the state). Actors who fulfil the roles of employee and client have to free themselves from

Lifeworld contexts and adapt to formally organised realms of action. The roles are juridically defined. This is not the case with the roles in the second category of exchange relations between System and Lifeworld, namely those of consumer and citizen, that is, participant in the formation of public opinion. The relevant juridical norms do not define these roles but only provide the scope, within which they can take shape on the basis of preferences and value orientations which have been formed in the private and public realm of the Lifeworld. These cannot be 'bought' as labour power or 'raised' as taxes.

Thus Habermas' 'working model' of advanced capitalist societies looks as follows from the perspective of the System:

Institutional orders of the Lifeworld	Interchange relations	Media-steered subsystems
Private sphere	1) P^1 ———→ labour power M ←——— Income from employment 2) M ←——— goods and services M^1 ———→ Demand	Economic system
Public sphere	1a) M^1 ———→ Taxes P ←——— Organisational accomplishments 2a) P ←——— Political decisions P^1 ———→ Mass loyalty	Administrative system

Source: Habermas, 1987:II 320

M = Money medium
P   = Power medium

The 'colonisation of the Lifeworld' comes about, as we saw above, when the steering media money and power penetrate, for reasons which we will look at below, into Lifeworld areas which require symbolic reproduction and thus remain dependent on communicative action. Everyday practice is then rationalised in such a one-sided fashion that a specialist-utilitarian style of life is established, in which consumerism and the individualism of property, achievement motivation and competition are predominant, and moral-practical elements have been forced out. The functional necessities of the systemically integrated realm are, if necessary, fulfilled at the cost of the 'technification' of the Lifeworld. This also implies that economy and state cannot be submitted to normative restrictions from the Lifeworld.

Why is this state of affairs not as clear to people in modern society as one would expect it to be? This is, says Habermas, because the disappearance of false consciousness has been followed by the coming about of fragmented consciousness. Let us first look at false consciousness. In politically stratified class societies the rationalisation of the domain of the sacred is, as it were, one phase behind that of the profane realm of everyday pratice. World views rooted in the domain of the sacred have less rationality but greater authority than the notions pertaining to everyday practice. The motives and value orientations based on these world views 'profit' from the immunity against dissonant experiences which these views owe to their rootedness in ritual and cultic practices. Religion and mythical world views can still have the functions of an ideology which veils the exploitation and repression which are characteristic for most class societies, though they are increasingly subject to the process which Habermas calls 'the linguistification of the sacred'.

This 'linguistification' amounts to a differentiation of the various formal world perspectives of the objective world, the social world of norms and values and the internal world and their appropriate validity claims. On a more concrete level it amounts to a differentiation of the various realms of discourse such as science and the humanities, the realm of morality and that of art. In the process art frees itself from its cultic origin, and morality and law from their religious and metaphysical background. Culture thus loses the properties which enabled it to fulfil ideological functions. It can no longer veil the structural violence of System imperatives which interfere in the forms of social integration. If this is the case one would imagine that the competition between forms of systemic and social integration would be open to view for everybody. Yet it is not so in the late capitalist welfare state. This is because rationalisation entails, with the *differentiation* of value spheres, also the *fragmentation* of everyday-consciousness. The differentiation of the realms of science and the humanities, morality and art has brought about expert subcultures which are cut off from everyday consciousness, and which no longer have a basis for unification, even in the form of false consciousness fed by ideology. Fragmented everyday consciousness is a functional equivalent for the preceding false consciousness, in the sense that it too is not able to clarify the thingification of the Lifeworld brought about by the predominance of systemic imperatives. The effects of the competition between forms of systemic and social integration are, to be sure, nefarious enough to be felt deeply, but they are not clear enough to be reduced to their causes. Habermas does not ascribe the obscurity of these matters to 'false consciousness' or ideology, which allegedly throws a veil over it. For ideology there is no longer a place in everyday communicative praxis. Thus the point is not that, via ideology, the *wrong* interpretation is given of these matters; the point is that, with a fragmented consciousness, the need for an interpretation is not even felt. Everyday consciousness is cut off from the culture of experts and thrown back on fragments of outworn traditions and religious and ideological cosmologies.

We find, at this point in Habermas' argument, the justification of the metaphor implicit in the term 'colonisation'. Habermas maintains that the imperatives of autonomous subsystems penetrate, when they have been stripped of their ideological veils, 'into the Lifeworld from the outside—like colonial masters coming into a tribal society—and force a process of assimilation upon it. The diffused perspectives of the local culture cannot be sufficiently coordinated to permit the play of the metropolis and the world market to be grasped from the periphery' (1987:II 355).

Though, as Habermas says, 'the play' cannot be seen through, yet the 'colonisation of the Lifeworld' evoked, and still does evoke, defensive reactions—in that sense too the term 'colonisation' is well chosen. In the course of recent history we have seen all kinds of minor and major revolts against the monetarisation of labour power and the bureaucratisation of the state's activities. Originally isolated defensive reactions, such as protests against taxes, price regulations, regulation of commercial activities and trade practices, are from the beginning of the nineteenth century replaced by the organised resistance of the labour movement. Yet the effectiveness of the new forms of organisation in the material reproduction of the Lifeworld ensured their survival.

We have indicated what the colonisation of the Lifeworld amounts to in terms of Habermas' general theoretical framework and provided some examples of it at the beginning of this chapter. We have not yet discussed, however, the alleged causes of this phenomenon. Why do the imperatives of the subsystems of economy and state administration penetrate, via the media of money and power, into the Lifeworld and bring about the pathologies which can be indicated with the general term 'thingification'?

This question can only be discussed in full when we look, in the second part of this book, at Habermas' comments on Weber and Marx. We will endeavour at this stage to sketch his own views independently from these comments. According to Habermas it is only when one also looks at the colonisation of the Lifeworld, as it takes place via the 'gateway' of power rather than just that of the market and money, that one can explain what, from an orthodox Marxist point of view, cannot be explained: the pacification of class conflict via the interventionism of the welfare state.

Yet Habermas' own recognition of the fact that this intervention is *necessary* from the point of view of the functional imperatives of the System is to him sufficient reason to call his approach, in spite of all of his criticisms of Marx, a Marxist one. The capitalist mode of production engenders different classes. Crises tendencies inherent in this mode of production would lead to acute class conflict if the roles of consumer and client, which market and state have brought about, did not constitute a form of compensation which tends to pacify conflict. This pacification, however, takes place at the price of the penetration of money and power into Lifeworld processes which remain dependent on the achievement of shared understanding via language. The colonisation of the Lifeworld implies its partial monetarisation and bureaucratisation, threatening its symbolic reproduction.

The state attempts to compensate for the functional deficiencies of the market without going to the extreme of having total state regulation of the economy. The state's interference amounts, rather, to the manipulation of marginal conditions for private entrepreneurial decisions and the implementation of strategies to avoid negative side effects of the unhampered functioning of the market.

The compensatory measures taken by the state do, however, not touch the basics of the structural inequalities in the distribution of property and income. Neither should the organisation and structure of economic production be affected. Class conflict can only be avoided under these circumstances if the state can use the increase in its social product for its compensatory measures. The state has, according to Habermas, been successful in this—and this is of course not in accord with orthodox Marxist theory—to the extent that the class structure has lost its historically concrete form, that is its 'Lifeworld form', and been shifted back into the economy, where it remains a matter of the unequal exchange between capital and labour. In the exchange between the economic system and the Lifeworld, the measures of the welfare state bring about a pacified world of labour which implies a new balance between a 'humanised' employee and a boosted consumer role—the one is acceptable because of the other. The counterpart to this is the neutralisation of the state citizen role, which is made acceptable because of an inflated client role.

But power needs legitimation, and under present circumstances this can only be bestowed on it by democratic procedures. There is, however, a tension between capitalism and democracy which cannot disappear, because both correlate with different forms of integration. Democracy implies the primacy of the Lifeworld and integration via communicative action, whereas capitalism requires that the subsystems can follow their own inner dynamics, are held free from legitimation requirements and fulfil their functional necessities, even at the cost of the technification of the Lifeworld.

Let us try to recapitulate all this within a paragraph or two. Capitalism remains a system of unequal exchange. Crises, originating within the economic system, and which are expressed in the Lifeworld as class conflict, threaten the possibilities for the legitimation of power and the motivation of actors which it needs for its continued functioning. Legitimation and motivation then have to be protected by the System's intervention through state power. Concretely, the state 'buys off' protest within the Lifeworld (that is, a possible threat to the legitimation of and motivation necessary for the System) through its compensatory measures. In doing so it interferes, by using law as a medium, in communicatively structured areas of the Lifeworld, such as primarily the private household, damaging in the process the cultural resources necessary for the continued existence of its symbolic structure. To refer to the examples we have given: family members cannot, at one and the same time, relate via communicative action and confront each other as legal subjects in an objectivating and instrumentalist disposition; the same remark holds for the relation between teachers and students.

We saw that to Habermas the term 'colonisation of the Lifeworld' refers to that pathology of modern society which 'the Greats' apprehended (and for which they used various terms such as alienation, rationalisation, 'the iron cage', anomie etc.) but which they could not adequately analyse. We will discuss, in the second part of this book, Habermas' comments on his great predecessors.

II
Habermas and the Great Theorists

6
Mead and Durkheim: The 'linguistification of the sacred'

In his magnum opus, *The Theory of Communicative Action*, Habermas presents his views partly through a history of theory, which is interwoven with the account of his own ideas. We have, however, for the sake of expository clarity, chosen to present Habermas' opinions on some of the great theorists separately here. Yet we would do scant justice to this part of his work if we suggested that it formed a merely illustrative exercise. Habermas would certainly not agree with this. The possibility of linking up his views to those of the great theorists constituted for him a sort of test. Social scientific paradigms are, as he sees it, directly related to the social context in which they come about. They serve the interpretation of specific social constellations of interests and originate within certain 'horizons of expectation and aspiration'. The more a body of theory can incorporate the intentions of earlier theoreticians and explain, criticise and continue the related theoretical traditions, the more it is protected against the risk that it merely expresses particular interests (Habermas, 1984a:I 140–41).

What Habermas says in a slightly different context about the coherence theory of truth applies here as well: 'The coherence theory of truth', he asserts 'is certainly too weak to explain the concept of propositional truth: but it comes into its own at another level, the metatheoretical, where we put together the individual pieces of theory like a puzzle' (Habermas, 1982:239). It is on this basis then that Habermas presents, sometimes in great detail, the ideas of Mead, Durkheim, Weber, Parsons and Marx and a host of lesser gods.

We stated in the first part of this book that to Habermas the fact that human beings communicate via language is decisive for the study of society. When he looks back through the history of sociological theory he encounters a theorist who focused on the same insight: George Herbert Mead. Habermas quotes Mead's statement that with human beings (as different from animals) functional differentiation through language creates a totally different principle of organisation, and thus a different type of society and individual. The German theorist finds in this American predecessor a social philosopher who had already made the changeover from the paradigm of the philosophy of consciousness to that of communications theory and centered upon symbolic interaction.

Mead pointed out that at the subhuman level communication could take place via gestures. We could think here, for instance, of the various stages of a dogfight, with its rituals of aggression and submission. At the human level interaction was symbolically mediated. Human beings communicated via signs of which the meaning was always dependent on a context. There were two main stages in this transition to symbolic interaction: the changeover from communication via gestures to communication via signs, and a second stage in which, with such activities as the hunt, territorial defence, sexual reproduction etc., coordination did not only come about via signs, but had also become normatively binding through social roles.

Habermas has objections to Mead's general account of the transition from the first to the second stage. Mead ignored the fact that action could be normatively regulated in different ways. The motivation to follow norms could be empirical but it could also be rational, that is, based on 'good reasons'. 'Good reasons' were formulated in claims to which people could take a critical stance. The possibility for making these claims and adopting that critical stance was based on a differentiation of language. But language is differentiated over time. How could action be normatively regulated at the stage when language was not yet differentiated and thus motivation had to be 'empirical'? Mead explained the occurrence of normatively regulated action from the child's capacity to take over the 'attitude of the generalised other'. In this process factually threatened, and sometimes exercised, group sanctions were internalised. Motivation through such internalised norms was predominantly 'empirical'. This process of internalisation, however, did not mean that the child merely followed norms because of a more or less realistic expectation of sanctions which would follow their violation. The norm was seen as having moral authority. Thus there was no mere compliance but obedience. Yet we cannot claim that motivation was entirely 'rational'. Before the growing child could ask the question, says Habermas, whether a norm was worthy of recognition, whether it was really in the interest of all those concerned, it had for him or her already been answered affirmatively. The elements of the general, in the 'generalised other', had mainly to do with internalised group sanctions. But there was also something else here. One element of the general was, already, the claim that a norm only deserved general validity to the extent that it was in the interest of all concerned and embodied the will of 'the generalised other', in the sense of the will of a group of which each member could represent his or her own interest. If 'the generalised other' mainly had this latter character the motivation for norm-regulated action would be predominantly 'rational' rather than 'empirical'. The full development of this form of 'the generalised other', however, required differentiation in language, which opened up possibilities for the exchange, to and fro, of claims which could be critically assessed. As said before, Mead has ignored this. In his account of the following of norms there was no distinction between 'empirical' and 'rational' motivation, between the stage in which the undifferentiated character of language still precluded the latter and the stage in which this had become possible. Also, why did Mead not look at the oldest manifestations of the authority of the generalised other, namely sacred symbols, to analyse the transition from just symbolic interaction to norm-regulated action? Mead has analysed the socialisation of the child in the group in which interaction is already norm-regulated, but there is no explanation of how the gap between the mere exchange of signs and the coordination of action on the basis of norms was bridged in the early stages of social evolution.

Habermas has another, perhaps even more weighty, objection to Mead. We saw that the American theorist explained how the child acquired the capacity for norm-regulated action. It was by 'taking the attitude of the generalised other'. But how do we explain the origination of the generalised other? Do we then again refer to the child's capacity for internalising norms, which ultimately brought about one of those adults whose action represented 'the generalised other' to other children? This would be a form of circular reasoning. The group must already have constituted itself as an entity, capable of action, before it could be regarded as a 'generalised other' which could exercise sanctions. What then could explain the social integration of such archaic groups? For an answer to this question

Habermas turns to a theorist who, in his view, has provided this, namely Mead's French contemporary, Emile Durkheim.

Durkheim saw this gap bridged in the sphere of the sacred. He pointed to the moral authority of norms in archaic societies. This authority had to be explained. It could not be explained by referring to the fact that these norms were enforced by external sanctions. This would merely be circular reasoning because the sanctions themselves were based on the norms. The right explanation had to be found in the analogy of the sphere of the moral with that of the sacred. In both spheres we would see the same ambiguous disposition, namely respect, bordering on fear, and desire. Durkheim concluded from this analogy the existence of a sacred basis of morality. The esteem for moral commands he understood, as he did the inner sanctions of shame and guilt following the infringement of moral rules, as the echo of older reactions rooted in the sphere of the sacred.

Durkheim dug deeper. He looked for the origin of the sacred and pointed out that religions consisted of beliefs and practices, and were the expression of a collective, supra-individual consciousness. But consciousness always had to be the consciousness of something. Of what in this case? The creed answered: of the divine being, of sacred powers etc. But behind these, said Durkheim, we find the transfigured and symbolically represented society. Habermas is not impressed by this explanation because he again finds a circular argument here. Moral authority is reduced to the sacred, this to the consciousness of an entity, namely society, which in its turn consists of a system of norms with moral authority. Yet this rather flawed logic has, according to Habermas, not prevented Durkheim from perceiving correctly that the integrative function of religion was mainly exercised via a collective attachment to material symbols, the totems, and that it was via these material signs that the believers could communicate their collective feelings. Their use allowed for an intersubjectivity which went beyond and above the primitive force of mutual suggestion, which could be found in any expression of feeling. Hence it was the existence of these symbols which made the coming about of a 'prelinguistic', normative, symbolically mediated consensus possible. It was via periodic ritual that the group 'recharged' these feelings of consensus.

When Habermas asks for the basis of this, he takes care not to commit what he believes to be Durkheim's error of referring to society; he points instead to the solidarity-creating energies of 'inborn programs' and behavourial dispositions which have their roots in basic instincts. These instincts are absorbed and 'sublimated' in symbols.

Habermas believes that Durkheim has given a satisfactory answer to the question of how normative consensus is reached and maintained in archaic societies, in which institutions have not yet separated themselves out in a process of differentiation and social roles and functions are structured through the kinship system. But what happens when this institutional differentiation is starting to come about? Durkheim has not really told us how consensus is reached and maintained then. And, apart from this problem of the social order, Durkheim has also not satisfactorily answered the second main question of classical social theory, namely that regarding the relation between the individual and society. How can the individuality of group members be understood when we adhere to Durkheim's views on collective identity?

To tackle the former question first, a differentiation of institutions will go together with a cognitive development in which Mead's level of symbolic interaction, in which mere signs are enough to release partly inborn, partly learned behavioural dispositions, is overcome. The linguistic expression of the new cognitive stage, in which actors are able to take an objectivating disposition towards a world of observable objects which can be manipulated, is found in the development of validity claims which refer to these objects and actors' intentions with them. But consensus about *these* types of claims is not enough as a basis for the coordination of action and thus, ultimately, for the social order. In fact 'cognitive transactions' with manipulable and observable objects and the expression of inner experience can already be found on the pre-linguistic level and have their roots in the animal realm. But normative consensus is brought about by symbolic means and Habermas maintains, against Durkheim, that the symbolic means found in ritual no longer suffice when some cognitive development has taken place and institutions have started to differentiate. He refers to Durkheim's distinction between the sacred and the profane to explain how, at this stage, normative consensus, and with it social solidarity, can be maintained. In the realm of the sacred religious symbols are not only linked to ritual but also to world views, as yet unchallenged via still-to-be-developed linguistic means for genuine discourse about other things than objects and intentions (it is, for the rest, Habermas' belief as we saw above, that the sacred retains an 'immunising' function also for a considerable time after these means have been developed). These world views link the identity of the group to the cosmic order.

World views are couched in language. Even though the realm of the sacred remains itself screened off from discourse in which normative claims can be fundamentally challenged, it can transmit its solidarity-creating energy to the newly differentiated institutions via linguistic means. In profane everyday practice people have to reach consensus about their situation in order to coordinate their actions. We have assumed that social development has led to a differentiation of institutions. This differentiation creates such a variety in everyday situations that people need the means to find out what situation they are actually in; they need the means to ascertain which specific norms hold for the specific situation; they need the means to find out what weight they should give to each other's claims, to what extent these are based on a genuine disposition. These means are linguistic. They consist, as we saw, of claims regarding the external world of objects, the social world of norms and the inner world of dispositions and feelings. Thus primeval religious solidarity is transmitted via world views, which are sorted out over the 'linguistic sorting machine', to various situations. This is what Habermas calls the 'linguistification of the sacred', a process in which the 'spellbinding and terrifying power of the sacred' is transformed into the 'binding/bonding force of criticisable claims to validity'. The 'linguistification of the sacred' increases, over time, in scope and intensity, leading to a rationalisation of world views and, ultimately, to the loss of their potency (Weber's process of disenchantment). When that stage has been reached the consensus necessary for the coordination of action should be reached, and potentially can be reached, through forms of discourse which, according to Habermas, Weber did not sufficiently consider. We will have a closer look at his criticism of Weber on this point at a later stage.

Now we will have a further look at Durkheim's position, as Habermas sketches it. Did the French theorist perceive something of this process of the linguistification of the sacred? Habermas maintains that he hovered on the brink of recognising it, that the whole idea is implicit in his views on the relation between religious thought and thought as such and that, in his sketch of the development of law, he depicted a specific form of it.

Let us first look at Durkheim's views on the relation between religious thought and thought as such. Habermas refers, on this topic, among other things, to the famous last chapter of Durkheim's *The Elementary Forms of the Religious Life,* where he finds the idea that normative consensus is, in its ideal form, above changes in space and time. This idea is the model for all notions of validity, says Habermas, and more specifically for that of truth. We find the element of a 'harmony of spirits' here, to which is added the idea of 'harmony with the nature of the case'. The idea of truth as the correspondence between propositions and facts is thus linked with the concept of an idealised consensus. On this basis the concept of a criticisable validity claim can originate (Habermas, 1987:II 72).

According to Habermas, Durkheim implicitly recognised the possibility of the 'linguistification of the sacred' in his views on the nature of the relation between idealised collective conceptions of the group and notions of validity. The French theorist sketched, in fact, this very process in his analysis of the development of law, as we can find this mainly in his book entitled *The Division of Labour in Society.* Durkheim saw criminal law as the most basic form of archaic law, and sacrilege as the most basic original crime. The condemnation of sacrilege was only the other side of the worship of the sacred. Hence criminal law was, in this view, in its origin basically religious and retained certain characteristics of this religiosity.

The typical form of modern law was, by contrast, civil law which focused on private property and, in relation to this, contract and inheritance. Modern law had lost the authority of the sacred. What had come in its place? Durkheim looked at this question mainly in the context of his observations on property and contract. Property was originally derived from the gods. Private property was merely a derived phenomenon. Contract was the central institution of modern law related to this. Durkheim's central question now was: how could contract have a binding character when the sacred foundation of law had fallen away? Could we explain this by merely referring to the compulsion exercised by the state? But that only shifted the question which then centered on the problem of how to explain the authority of the political order. What was Durkheim's answer to these questions? Habermas summarises it as follows: contracts only have an obligatory character because of the legitimacy of the regulations on which they are based. These regulations can only be taken as legitimate if they express a general interest. The general interest owes its morally binding force to the fact that it is impersonal and non-partisan. The collective consciousness in differentiated societies is embodied in the state. Its legitimacy is no longer based on 'the sacred', but forged, and clarified, in general discourse. The purest example of this state of affairs is found in modern democracy.

Habermas sees in all this clearly a sketch of the 'linguistification of the sacred'. 'As we have seen', he says, 'in his later writings, particularly in his studies of the sociology of religion and law, Durkheim came close to the idea of the linguistification of a basic religious consensus that has been set communicatively aflow' (Habermas, 1987:II 85–86).

Why then did he not fully attain this idea? It is in the answer to this question that Habermas' major difference, not only with Durkheim but also with Weber and to a lesser extent Marx, is found. We have commented on this before as far as Weber is concerned. Let us now look at Durkheim.

Compared to Habermas Durkheim had a narrow view of rationality and scientific procedure. His famous statement that 'social facts are things' implied the exhortation to treat them as externally observable and quantifiable matters. It also implied a thorough demarcation of the scientific realm of sociology from the everyday realm of 'common sense', which was, to him, not marked by its potential for rationality but rather by all kinds of prejudices. The process of cognition was to Durkheim too a matter of (an isolated) subject perceiving an object from outside. The rationality of scientific procedure was, in the first place, a matter of the quality of subject–object relations rather than the (potential) rationality of subject–subject relations, in which consensus is reached about what should provisionally be accepted as a scientific result. Durkheim did not focus on the (potential) rationality of subject–subject relations in the scientific realm, and he certainly did not do so as far as the realm of everyday life was concerned. He refused to take his point of departure in sociological explanation from action, because action was to him not, basically, interaction, but action of the solitary ego whose individual intentions could only be marked by the waywardness and irrationality of that what was really individual in him, that is, 'organo-physical' man.

Habermas cannot accept this. We saw earlier that he believes that Durkheim has not given a satisfactory account of the relation between society and individual. Let us have a closer look at this.

Habermas quotes Durkheim's statement in which the latter asserted that we find in Man an individual being, which has its basis in the organism, and a social being, which represents society in us. Durkheim identified this duality with that of sensations and sensual appetites on the one hand and concepts and morality on the other. But it is clear, says Habermas, that he still remained imprisoned here within the philosophy of consciousness. The distinction he made between states of the individual and those of the collective consciousness was really a distinction between such states *within* an individual consciousness.

Habermas finds this unsatisfactory and points to the contrast with Mead who, as we know, divided the self up into an 'I' and a 'Me' (which Habermas identifies with Freud's concepts 'ego' and 'superego'), which *both* emerged from social interaction. The principle of individualisation did not, for Mead, rest on the body, but on a structure of perspectives given with communicative action. A participant in such action could react, either positively or negatively, to a validity claim. The freedom to do either one or the other constituted individuality. The 'I' stood for this freedom. 'Self', said Mead, was in fact a social process of which 'Me' and 'I' were the different phases (quoted in Habermas, 1987:II 59). The structure of linguistic intersubjectivity, so Habermas maintains, exerts imperceptible pressure for individualisation on the person who is growing up. Here too the energy of social solidarity branches out via communicative action, but now we look at it from the point of view of socialisation rather than action coordination. Mead's 'I' is in Habermas' terminology the world of subjective experience to which the individual has privileged access. That world can only come about in a process in which it gets separated from the other worlds—the objective and the social. The increasing capacity to keep these worlds apart is obtained through the process of growing up, that is of socialisation.

Mead managed to combine, because he took his analytic point of departure from language, what Durkheim could not bring together: the explanation of the origin of individuality with that of the maintenance and re-creation of society. Durkheim's deficiency on this score had the same source as his inability to grasp fully the process of the 'linguistification of the sacred', namely what is to Habermas an inadequate epistemology, and the concomitant narrow idea of rationality, inherent in the 'philosophy of consciousness'. Durkheim shared this alleged inadequacy with Weber, at whose view of rationalisation, in Habermas' account of it, we will now have a closer look.

7
The 'linguistification of the sacred' and Weber's rationalisation thesis

We saw, in the previous chapter, that Habermas could draw on Durkheim for the view that social solidarity is, in an early stage of social evolution, based on a collective attachment to material symbols of the sacred. This attachment leads to 'pre-linguistic' feelings of consensus which can be 'recharged' in periodic ritual. With the increasing differentiation of society social solidarity acquires a different basis. In a process which Habermas calls the 'linguistification of the sacred', such solidarity is increasingly based on the binding and bonding force of argument. Though Durkheim had, according to Habermas, some inkling of this process he failed to give a proper account of it.

In the first part of this book we analysed Habermas' views on the binding force of argument. We saw that it depended on communicative rationality, the capacity to provide, and be receptive to, good reasons for claims concerning the objective, social and subjective world. Thus the 'linguistification of the sacred' is also a matter of the coming about of clear distinctions between the three formal world concepts, and the appropriate validity claims, through the differentiation of the mythical/religious world views in which these concepts were originally fused. Habermas finds an analysis of this process, and an indication of what set it going, in Weber, who coined the term 'rationalisation' for it.

In the case of Weber too, Habermas presents his own views while at the same time critically pruning and reshaping those of his great predecessor. This is so much the case that it becomes difficult to identify what Habermas owes to Weber here or, leaving matters of intellectual debt aside, where we find substantial agreement between the views of the two theorists in their treatment of this theme. The answer to this question is that this can mainly be found in their sharing, up to a point, a general perspective on the importance of the differentiation of religious world views and the factors playing a part in this.

Habermas' main disagreement with Weber on this topic can be found in a direction which is by now familiar to us. He deems Weber's concept of rationality, here as well, to be too narrow, in any case at certain stages of his analysis. In the transition from the analysis of the rationalisation of culture, as we find this especially in Weber's sociology of religion, to that of society, he allegedly narrowed down his concept of rationality. He analysed the process of religious 'disenchantment' or 'demagification', which created the internal conditions for the manifestation of Western rationalism, with the aid of a complex, though rather unclarified, concept of rationality. But when it then came to the matter of the rationalisation of society, he was mainly guided by the limited idea of goalrationality. When Weber studied the links between the rationalisation of culture and that of society he concentrated in his research, says Habermas, on the 'moral practical' foundation of the institutionalisation of goalrational action (Habermas, 1984a:I 143–44, 155).

Thus here too the basic disagreement between Weber and Habermas has ultimately to do with the differences in their conception of action. Habermas seems to suggest that, since to Weber the rationality of action was primarily a matter of goalrationality, the latter has 'tuned' his analysis of rationalisation in such a fashion that he found the institutionalisation of this type of rationality as the sole outcome of it, at any case in the West. We have made clear, in the first part of this book, how, in Habermas' view, this narrow conception of the rationality of action is tied up to a certain philosophical paradigm, namely that of the philosophy of consciousness.

We return to the basic agreement in the views of these two theorists, which we said was, among other things, a matter of general perspective. This perspective concerns the process of the differentiation of world views which is at the basis of the creation of separate realms of discourse for science and technology, for art and for morality and law. However, Weber talked here of 'value spheres', which all developed according to their own logic and between which, in the course of their development, tension steadily increased. Habermas looks at the process of differentiation on a higher level of abstraction, talks of the coming about of formal world concepts and stresses the unity in the formal properties of thought pertaining to different domains.

Thus, in identifying a similarity in perspective, we cannot avoid signalling, at the same time, some basic differences in outlook. How does Habermas explain this difference in detail, apart from his fundamental objection to the narrowness of Weber's concept of rationality? According to him Weber underestimated the extent to which rationality and rationalisation share the same formal properties in different cultures and in different so-called value spheres of the same culture, because he did not distinguish clearly enough between these formal properties and the contents of rationalisation. Habermas believes that it was mainly because this clear distinction was lacking that Weber underestimated the universal character of rationality.

He is of the opinion that the rationalisation of *any* religious world view can lead to the differentiation of the three world perspectives, the external world of objective facts, the social world of values and norms and the internal world of inner states and feelings. The extent to which this happens is due to fortuitous historical circumstances. Can he find the same view in Weber? He cannot answer this question with an unqualified yes.

Is rationalisation a universal phenomenon or, to make this question more specific, has rationalisation as we find it in the West universal significance? Anyone who has read the first sentence of Weber's introduction to his famous treatise on the protestant ethic knows that he answered these questions in an ambiguous fashion. He said there that 'we like to think' that the developments summarised under the term rationalisation have universal significance, without committing himself to an answer to the question of whether or not we are right in thinking so.

Habermas recognises this ambiguity. At the same time he emphasises that it is clear from Weber's conceptual approach that he really took a 'universalist position' on this matter. This approach made it to Weber too an inevitable conclusion, though he did not come up with this himself, that even though the spheres of scientific thought, post-traditional legal and moral views and autonomous art (we do recognise here Habermas' three worlds) can have different *contents* in different cultures, they yet share the same formal properties. Weber did not, however, clarify this matter sufficiently. He emphasised that life can be rationalised from different ultimate points of view and into different directions and that, accordingly, what is rational from one point of view can be irrational from another. But here again he seemed to confuse, according to Habermas, the cultural contents with formal properties. When for instance Weber argued that the rationalisation of warfare or the administration of justice or education could seem to be, when regarded from other spheres of life, specifically irrational, he was really talking about the relative significance of such a field of action in the whole of culture. He was not speaking of the technologies which are applied in these processes of rationalisation, technologies of which the formal properties might be more or less similar. If the whole of a society is geared to warfare, as has happened in certain periods of the history of Sparta or, more recently, Prussia, this might seem from the point of view of the economy, for instance, irrational. Yet rather similar techniques are followed in the rationalisation of warfare and of the economy.

Habermas admits that when Weber spoke of 'ultimate points of view' he was not always talking about the cultural contents of the various spheres of life. On occasion he also referred to the abstract ideas behind these spheres: such ideas as truth behind the cognitive value sphere; normative rightness behind the practical value sphere; beauty, authenticity, sincerity behind the expressive value sphere (again we recognise Habermas' three worlds). It was Weber's conviction that each of these value spheres followed their own laws in their own processes of rationalisation, that they were inherently irreconcilable, and that this irreconcilability became more and more apparent with further rationalisation. Anyone who has read Weber's famous 'Zwischenbetrachtung', which in its English version appeared under the title 'Religious Rejections of the World and Their Directions' in Gerth and Mills' well-known anthology of Weber (Gerth and Mills, 1957:129–56), has encountered this Weberian idea. Habermas' argument against this more basic view is that Weber has not really proven that these value spheres *as such* are irreconcilable. Is this whole problem not rather a matter of the unbalanced growth of certain areas of life such as, for instance, in our society, the growth of the capitalist economy and modern administration, at the expense of others?

Habermas' argument here, as elsewhere, is that though Weber has recognised in his *substantive studies* that the rationalisation of originally religious world views is ultimately a matter of the differentiation of (Habermas') three formal world perspectives, he has not made this sufficiently clear on the metatheoretical level. He allegedly kept confusing the rationalisation of the cultural contents of a sphere of life with the differentiation of the formal world perspectives into which these fit, and with the formal-operational aspects of thought which have led to this differentiation.

Here of course we are on an important point for Habermas. The issue is always the same: the delineation and defence of a wide concept of rationality, or, as he put it in the title of a recent article, the 'unity of Reason in the multiplicity of its voices'. This unity, it is again clear from his remarks on Weber, should be found in the formal properties of discourse.

The 'universalism' of Habermas' views on rationalisation depends not only on this alleged identity of the formal properties of thought but also on his obvious conviction that the three formal world concepts, those of the objective, the social and the subjective world, are not just the fortuitous outcome of Western developments. The rationalisation of any religious world views could, potentially, lead to them. In addition he seems to accept Weber's claim that a similar problem is at the origin of this process of rationalisation, namely the problem of the theodicy. Weber saw this problem come about not only where, with the conception of one universal God, above this world, the question arose of how the omnipotence of such a God could be in accordance with the imperfections of the world he had created, but also in cultures where the conception of an impersonal but meaningful world order prevailed. He maintained that 'in some variety or other the problem is everywhere among the determinants of religious development and the need for salvation' (Weber, 1922:297).

If the formal properties of thought are similar, regardless of the cultural contents of rationalisation processes; if, also, the development of the three formal world concepts can be the outcome of the rationalisation of any religious world view; if, furthermore, a similar problem constitutes the point of departure for processes of rationalisation, two problems seem to follow. How can we explain the obvious differences in the outcome of rationalisation processes and how do we account, specifically, for the development in the West? As far as the first problem is concerned Habermas suggests that research on this point should be guided by the clear distinction between, on the one hand, the direction of religious development (which can be explained by reference to the core problem and the structures of world views) and on the other the actual realisation of structurally circumscribed possibilities (which has to do with external factors) (cf. Habermas, 1984a:196–97). We recognise here the distinction between the logic and the dynamics of development.

Weber has not, Habermas suggests, especially in his study of rationalisation in the West, followed this distinction with enough consistency. In his study of Western developments he concentrated first on the ethical aspect of rationalisation (that is on one of the world perspectives), studying this mainly in its form of the institutionalisation of law which, moreover (an even further narrowing of Weber's focus), was considered to be largely the embodiment of goalrationality. Because of these unwarranted constrictions of his thesis Weber, according to Habermas, did not ask two vital questions: a) which forms of rationalisation would have been *possible* in the West (as distinct from the rationalisation which actually did take place) and b) which other forms of rationalisation *did* actually take place (as apart from those which Weber indicated) (cf. Habermas, 1984a:221–22).

We can, on the basis of what has been said in previous chapters, understand that these questions are vital to Habermas because they are central to the theory of society as a critical enterprise. Criticism requires the indication, either explicitly or implicitly, of other possibilities.

The guiding thread which Weber did follow in his inquiries on rationalisation, that of the dialectic of interests and ideas, was, again, not followed consistently enough, says Habermas, to prevent his identification of what he believed to be the actual form of rationalisation in the West with rationalisation as such. Weber indicated the nature of the relation between interests and ideas in the following famous statement: 'It is interests . . . not ideas which dominate the action of human beings. But the "world views" created by "ideas" have often determined, as switchmen, the lines along which action was pushed by the dynamics of interests.' Neither interests nor ideas could by themselves effect social change, that is change in the 'legitimate order' in which interests and ideas were combined. Interests could in the long run only be satisfied, via the norms which regulate social relations, when they were connected with ideas which serve as the basis of these norms. Ideas could not be realised empirically when they were not related to interests which gave them power (cf. Habermas, 1984a:I 187ff.). The implementation of ideas depended on the groups which carried them (*Trägerschichten*). The crucial role in real innovations, under changed external circumstances, was, furthermore, played by charismatic figures who had a great capacity for creating new 'meaning', that is, new frames of reference. One can think here, in the first place, of the great founders of the world religions. Only in a later stage we saw the intellectual elaboration of the new ideas by the professional 'literati', priests, monks, teachers of wisdom, etc. It was their intellectual activities which were guided by that imperative of consistency, which Weber noticed as a general feature of the process of rationalisation.

Habermas' comment on this general framework is that we should make a distinction between the interplay of ideas and interests on the level of society, where they are at the basis of the institutionally ordered realms of life, and this same interplay on the level of culture. This two-pronged approach can indeed be found in Weber. However, Habermas believes that we should go further. We should, as far as culture is concerned, also distinguish between such developments as seem to be *possible* within certain world-view structures and those developments which *actually* take place. In other words, here again we have a warning to keep the 'logic' and the 'dynamics' of development strictly separate.

Habermas believes that here as elsewhere Weber did not keep these matters clearly apart. He did not make enough distinction between the particular solutions of the particular problem (that of the theodicy) which was at the basis of rationalisation, and the 'general structures of consciousness' which came about in the process. With the term 'structures of consciousness' Habermas is referring here to the three formal world concepts he sees coming about as a result of rationalisation. Their clear separation as we already saw, is to him a matter of the 'logic' of rationalisation because the potential for the development of these perspectives is to be found in the human capacity for rationality in and through language. The particular way in which the problem of the theodicy is worked out, in the process of rationalisation, is also influenced by external factors and is thus a matter of the 'dynamics' of development as well. Such external factors are, for instance, constituted by the social structural situations which provide the 'setting' for a theodicy problem, or by the social 'carriers' of the rationalisation of a new world view etc. It is factors such as these which explain the original *impetus* to the unfolding of world-view structures, as well as the *selective use* of the possibilities in the coming about of the actual contents of world views.

Habermas argues that if Weber had followed this two-tiered approach consistently enough he could have reasoned that, given the presence of certain interests in the societies he was dealing with, cultural rationalisation, that is the rationalisation of ideas, only had certain limited chances to become socially effective, that is to contribute to the rationalisation of society. In other words, he would then have asked, which specific interests were responsible for the fact that cultural rationalisation came about in a selective way. Weber allegedly did not ask this. Moreover, even in his account of what actually happened he focused unduly, as we saw, on the element of goalrationality. This can, it is true, on the one hand be explained from the real importance which the institutionalisation of goalrational action has for modern society. But on the other hand it should be recognised that this restriction of focus was *also* due to the limitations inherent in Weber's particular conception of action with its emphasis on goalrationality. Cultural rationalisation in the West did, according to Habermas, have other aspects, aspects which have also become socially effective but which Weber under-emphasised or ignored.

> ... he began with the fact that the purposive rationality of entrepreneurial activity was institutionalized in the capitalist enterprise and believed that the explanation of this fact provided the key to the explanation of capitalist modernization ... Weber explains the institutionalization of purpose-rational economic action first by way of the Protestant vocational culture and subsequently by way of the modern legal system ... With them arises a new form of social integration that can satisfy the functional imperatives of the capitalist economy. Weber did not hesitate to equate *this* particular historical form of rationalization with rationalization of society *as such*. (Habermas, 1984a:I 221)

Let us have a closer look at these matters in the following two chapters.

8

The protestant ethic and the spirit of capitalism: Weber's generalisation from one historical case

In his comments on Weber's famous thesis Habermas focuses on an aspect which is often overlooked, namely the fact that the 'protestant ethic thesis' also contains the view that in the modern era the rationality which was reinforced at the beginning of modern capitalism by the protestant ethic survives in the form of secular utilitarianism. He pictures the main difference between his and Weber's view on this matter, as we saw, as follows. For Weber the development from protestant ethic to secular utilitarianism was the only possible one. For Habermas there were other possibilities, some of which were realised. In this chapter we will look at the details of Habermas' argument on this point.

Let us first look at the following question: how and why can the protestant ethic be at the basis of a rationality which in more recent times can only be found in a secular context? In order to make this clear we have to look closely (in fact more closely than Habermas does) at Weber's notion of the historical distinction between the ethics of internal and the ethics of external relations. When this distinction prevailed, commercial transactions within what the older American sociology called the face-to-face group, especially the family, were governed by an ethic which was different from the ethic which prevailed in the transactions with outsiders. One could say that the ideal pattern within the face-to-face group was based on what Weber called the 'ethics of brotherhood', whereas the dealings members of this group had with outsiders were based on an 'unscrupulous' cutthroat ethic. It was Weber's view that, for the neutral impersonality of modern market transactions to come about, the distinction between those two types of ethics had to disappear. Central to his idea of modern capitalism was the importance of 'calculability' in rational capital accounting. This

84

calculability would not exist if the way people dealt with each other in the market differed from case to case.

Weber emphasised, especially in the famous 'Zwischenbetrachtung', that in both religion and the market there was a push for the abolition of the distinction between the ethics of internal and the ethics of external relations, but they pushed in opposite directions as it were. The thrust of religion was to extend the ethic of internal relations outside the kin group, whereas the logic of the market implied that the 'cold impersonality' of transactions (the basis of calculability) should also prevail within the face-to-face group.

How then could there ever be an ethical basis for that 'cold impersonality' of the market and the systematic goalrational conduct which went with it? It seems that that ethical basis, at least its historical roots, could only be found in religion, but we just saw that religion, according to Weber's analysis, promoted the 'ethics of brotherhood' rather than the cold impersonality of market transactions. Here is where the protestant ethic comes in as a special case. When Weber talked about protestantism within the context of his famous thesis, he was really referring to Calvinism. The peculiarity of Calvinism was, however, that its theology provided the basis not for an ethics of brotherhood but an ethics which stressed the importance of the methodical conduct of the elect. Those who were saved were not saved on the basis of their works (they could only be recognised as belonging to the elect on the basis of these) but would, as a 'tool of the divine Will', methodically serve the divine order within an earthly setting. Calvinism provided the ethical basis for goalrational conduct on the basis of a (secular) calling.

It is within this context that we should understand Schluchter's interpretation of Weber's thesis (referred to by Habermas) according to which protestantism made possible the idea of being a child of God, but not that of a community of God. Exactly because this form of protestantism knew a 'monological' ethic with 'unbrotherly consequences' it could be at the basis of modern developments.

The words 'at the basis' should be emphasised here, because, in the long run, the subsystems of goalrational action provided a destructive environment for the protestant ethic. Why was this so? Puritan protestantism too had elements which were inimical to 'modernity'. From the point of view of scientifically rational schemes of interpretation of the world this form of religion too remained irrational. Religious schemes of interpretation focus on a 'meaning' in history which remains, somehow, in accordance with ethical postulates (though, here too, Calvinism deviated more from the ideal type than most other brands of Christianity). However, the 'ethical neutrality' of the 'modern scientific world view' is, of necessity, inimical to all religion.

If we want to put this in terms of Weber's well-known distinction between 'goalrationality' and 'value rationality' we get the following account. The 'goalrational' character of action is determined by the adequacy of means to a certain ('ethically neutral') end: its value-rational character is determined by the consistency of its relation to a certain value. Value rationality is closely tied up to religion. Thus the modern, scientific, 'ethically neutral' world view is conducive to the 'one-sided' development of goalrationality.

The unsatisfactory element in this account, to Habermas, is that Weber depicted what is basically a fortuitous Western historical development as a necessary development, or, in terms of Habermas' terminology, did not make a sufficiently sharp distinction between the 'logic' and the 'dynamics' of development. Weber, says Habermas, has not really given us any proof that rationalisation as such makes value rationality, a moral consciousness based on principles, impossible. He hasn't really established that such a consciousness can only survive in and through religion. The fact that this consciousness *originated* within salvation religion does not imply that it can only *survive* within this context.

Weber's account will be found to be deficient when we look at both the 'logic' and the 'dynamics' of development. As far as its *logic* is concerned, the coming about of a secular ethic is consistent with the rationalisation of religious world views. As far as the *dynamics* are concerned, Habermas points to various historical facts which Weber allegedly more or less ignored and which, according to Habermas, make it clear that ethical rationalisation can go together with a variety of historical contexts. He argues that Groethuysen's inquiry into the origination of the bourgeois world view in France demonstrated that a principle-guided ethics could also come about and exist in a secular context. Furthermore, Habermas points to certain directions in modern philosophy which deal in a systematic fashion with moral-practical questions. Third, it is simply not true that rationalisation as such has been historically incompatible with the ethics of brotherhood. Here Habermas points to a historical attempt to push the ethics of brotherhood beyond the confines of the family group in a consistent manner, namely that of the Anabaptists. (Habermas is probably referring here to the radically egalitarian and 'anarchist' religious movement which originally conquered Munster and then was drowned in blood (1539). Its egalitarian principles survived in the far less radical Baptist church founded by Menno Simons.)

Weber allegedly 'missed' these things because of his tendency to identify rational action with goalrational action. This was related to his conviction that ethical value judgments only expressed subjective dispositions and were ultimately a matter of 'decisions'. They were thus not the outcome of rational discourse. Hence the realm of norms and values could hardly be subject to a process of rationalisation. Habermas' position is, as we saw, that 'communicative rationality' not only plays a role in discourse concerning the truth of factual propositions, but also in that regarding the 'rightness' of normative statements (this view is particularly noticeable in his treatment of Weber's sociology of law which we will deal with in the following chapter).

Because Weber did not sufficiently separate the 'logic' and the 'dynamics' of the development which he called rationalisation, he allegedly failed to identify the real historical cause of the fact that what Habermas calls cognitive-instrumental rationality, and what Weber calls most often goalrationality, has indeed penetrated many areas of life. Weber thought that this was just a matter of this type of rationality providing scope for superior efficiency. Habermas argues that the real cause is deeper. It has to be found in the nature of capitalism itself.

Our concern here is not with the tenability or otherwise of Habermas' views on Weber. Our concern is to understand what the former is driving at. When we want to indicate what Habermas has in mind here we have to go back to the three concepts which, as we saw, are pivotal to his sociology: 'communicative action', 'Lifeworld' and 'System'. Habermas' thesis on social evolution in the West is, as we will remember, roughly as follows: the rationality of 'communicative action' is based on the more or less free exchange and criticisability of validity claims. The principles on which it is based are identical to those of democracy and egalitarianism. Capitalism is inimical to democracy and egalitarianism. It does not fit into the 'Lifeworld', which is integrated by communicative action, but into the 'System', which is integrated by such media as money and power. Modernisation does not just mean an increasing prevalence of goalrationality, as Weber had it, but a disjunction of 'System' and 'Lifeworld' and an increasing penetration of the latter by the former, the process in short, which Habermas calls the 'colonisation of the Lifeworld'.

Weber did not use the same dramatic term but he did speak of 'loss of meaning' and 'loss of freedom' as consequences of rationalisation. One could in general say that Habermas agrees with Weber's analysis here. What he cannot find in Weber, however, is an adequate analysis of the causes of the social pathologies for which he himself has coined the term 'colonisation'. Let us have a closer look at this.

We are by now familiar with Habermas' interpretation of Weber's thesis on the loss of meaning in modern society. For Weber the weakening of religion and metaphysics led to the gradual disappearance of the unifying force of collective convictions. Most of us are familiar with the image he evoked in this context in one of his last public speeches, 'Scholarship as a Vocation', where he spoke of the old gods which have risen from their graves and have resumed their age-old struggle. This antagonism of ultimate value spheres could not be solved via reason which, in Weber's view, was basically cognitive-instrumental and was thus a matter of goal-rationality. This goalrationality also provided the ultimate orientation to a rationalised bureaucracy whose arrangements and regulations entrapped the people of today as in an 'iron cage'.

To Weber rationalisation and secularisation, the demagification or disenchantment he referred to in so many places of his work, were two sides of the same coin. And since rationalisation meant to him the increasing prevalence of goalrationality, the suggestion was created that a secular value rationality had no chance of existence. We saw that to Habermas, who referred on this point to Groethuysen's study on the origination of the bourgeois world view, this amounts to an incorrect reading of the historical facts. A secularised form of a 'principle-guided moral consciousness' does exist, though this took root at first only in certain social layers. The development of these forms of universalist law and morality is, to Habermas, not just a matter of the coming about of ideological reflexes of the capitalist mode of production. It is, rather, the consequence of a collective learning process of which the results cannot be undone, only repressed. The fact that allegedly Weber did not adequately perceive this phenomenon also led to his misinterpretation, Habermas says, of rationalisation in law as an increase in goalrationality, his misconception of 'material rationality' as mainly an interruption and disturbance of the legal rationalisation process and his inadequate perception of the real basis of legitimation in our society.

For Habermas the rationalisation of action systems can, as we saw, only be adequately analysed on the basis of a more complex concept of rationality than we find in Weber, a concept which includes besides the cognitive-instrumental aspect of rationality, also its moral-practical and aesthetic-expressive aspects. This allows for the clear distinction between the rationalisation of communicative action and that of the subsystems of goalrational economic and administrative action. It also allows for a shift of the analysis of modern social pathologies from the level of conflicting action orientations to that which focuses on conflicting principles of societal integration.

We saw that to Habermas this conflict between different principles of integration ends with the undue predominance of systemic integration—the loss of meaning and of freedom which Weber signalled but could not adequately explain. Systemic integration and systemic rationality were beyond Weber's ken since, on the basis of his action theory, he still pictured the action of organisations as a mere extension of the goalrational action of its members. In social scientific functionalism this point of view has been abandoned, because the self-steering capacities of systems cannot be explained from the goalrational disposition of individuals participating in it. Habermas believes that Weber somehow adumbrated the distinction between systemic rationality and goal-rationality in his metaphor for the modern bureaucracy, which he compared with a living machine. To Habermas this is indeed the proper metaphor for formally organised realms of action, which are not integrated through action oriented to the achievement of shared understanding, that is, communicative action, and thus 'crystallise' into a kind of norm-free sociality. This formal organisation is only possible on the basis of a thoroughgoing rationalisation, and thus differentiation of the Lifeworld, of which one aspect is the separation between morality and legality. In this way a basis is created for the juridical arrangements underlying the new formal organisation.

The undue predominance of these arrangements, and with it the undue predominance of systemic over social integration, cannot merely be explained, as Weber is inclined to do, from those new organisations' effectiveness and the appreciation of this in a general 'secularized' mental climate in which goalrationality has come to prevail over value rationality. First, Habermas argues, secularisation has not excluded the rationalisation of moral-practical and aesthetic-expressive aspects. Second, from the perspective of the Lifeworld this undue predominance of systemic integration is perceived as a threat. The rationalisation of the Lifeworld has provided chances for self-expression, the 'moral-practical formation of the will' and aesthetic satisfaction which cannot be used. Thus not only social integration is threatened but also the socialisation and identity formation of individuals. Weber had an open eye for the paradoxes of rationalisation but he saw them, Habermas believes, as 'in a glass darkly'. He could not properly analyse, for the reasons indicated above, the real causes of the 'colonisation of the Lifeworld'. For hints (and not more than that) regarding the proper analysis of this Habermas believes we should turn to Marx. We will deal with Habermas' views on Marx in due course, but before we do so we should have a closer look at the second major aspect of Habermas' critical comment on Weber's rationalisation thesis, namely his strictures on Weber's sociology of law.

9
Weber and the rationalisation of law

Habermas analyses Weber's views on the rationalisation of law along the same lines as he did the latter's famous thesis on the protestant ethic. Again he believes he can establish that Weber wrongly equated rationalisation with an increase in goalrationality and that this alleged error is mainly due to his theory of action, which led to a lack of historical attention to developments in other dimensions of rationality.

Weber saw among the historical conditions for capitalism the coming about of the protestant ethic and a modern system of law, says Habermas. With these a moral consciousness based on principles could be embodied in the personality system and the institutional system. Thus goalrational action orientations were firmly anchored in value rationality.

Though this was Weber's own line of analysis, Habermas continues, he nevertheless looked at the rationalisation of society exclusively from the point of view of goalrationality. 'Only the cognitive-instrumental complex of rationality acquires significance for the rationality of action systems.' Thus processes of rationalisation seemed, ultimately, merely matters of empirical-theoretical knowledge and the instrumental and strategic aspects of action.

Habermas believes that he can see this alleged internal contradiction in Weber's thought clearly in the latter's sociology of law in which modern law is, on the one hand, conceived of as ultimately finding its roots in moral-practical rationality, but yet is also seen as 'a parallel case to the embodiment of cognitive-instrumental rationality in the economy and the state administration ...' (Habermas, 1984a:I 254).

He backs up this interpretation of Weber's views with a few

quotations from him. In one of these Weber stated that jurisprudence only indicated where and when certain rules of law, and
certain methods of its interpretation, should be applied. But
jurisprudence did not, Weber said, answer the question whether
there should be law, or these particular rules of law, at all. 'It can
only state: If one wishes this result, according to the norms of our
legal thought this legal rule is the appropriate means of getting it.'
Here Habermas finds the idea that law can, like the economy or the
state, be formally rationalised with reference to the relations of ends
and means 'from a particular value standpoint' (1984a:I 252).
Another statement of Weber seems to lend even more plausibility to
Habermas' interpretation of his views, namely that in which Weber
spoke of the inevitable fate of law of becoming a rational apparatus,
without inner sanctity, and liable to be transformed at any
particular moment in a goalrational way (1984a:I 268).

Weber's alleged tendency to shift attention from the value-
rational foundation of goalrational economic and administrative
action to the goalrational applicability of juridical means of
organisation is for Habermas particularly visible in three lines of
Weber's argument, namely in his interpretation of rational natural
law, in his positivistic equation of legality and legitimacy, and in his
view of the 'substantive rationalisation' of law as a threat to its
formal qualities. We will look at each of these points in turn.

The argument about natural law is an intricate one and we could
not possibly do justice here to the details of Habermas' view or to
Weber's for that matter. Let us first see what the concept of natural
law stands for and then indicate Habermas' main line of reasoning
on this point. Natural law is that law of which the principles are dis-
cernible to reason, and it is therefore distinguished from law which
owes its validity to the mere fact of being codified. Habermas'
interpretation of Weber's views on natural law is that the latter saw
this type of law on the one hand as providing the link between the
ideas of legitimacy and rational agreement but on the other as
exactly therefore not a part of modern law. Weber understood
modern law, says Habermas, in positivistic fashion, as law which
needed no other foundation than the decision of the legislature
(Habermas, 1984a:I 263). Habermas calls this view 'positivistic'
because in legal positivism the element of human creation in law is
absolutised; law is, in this view, that which is enacted by the
legislator and administered by courts, quite apart from its contents.
The question whether these are 'moral' or 'immoral' is, from the
juridical point of view, irrelevant.

Habermas' second point is related to the previous one and has to do with Weber's identification of legality and legitimacy. If the continued existence of a political order always requires legitimacy, that is, the belief among rulers and ruled alike that this authority is somehow justified, how then can such legitimacy be established in modern Western society? In Weber's answer to this question, which issued in his ideal type of 'legal-rational authority', Habermas again sees signs of Weber's alleged legal positivism. Weber's legal-rational authority found the basis for its legitimacy in the correct observance of the procedures prescribed for its exercise. Hence the necessity for the moral-practical foundation of legal norms was totally lost sight of, and legality was equated with legitimacy. Habermas believes that there is an obvious vicious circle here because the legitimacy of authority was supposed to be based on the following of rules which had been established by this authority in the first place. The ideal type of legal-rational authority fitted in with Weber's alleged view that the rationalisation of law was really a matter of goalrationality, that it had mainly to do with the law's usefulness as a technical apparatus in the realisation of goals set outside the law, for instance by the market or bureaucratic administration.

Weber did not sufficiently recognise, says Habermas, that the rationalisation of law could only take place on the basis of a 'post-traditional' development of moral consciousness, which came about through the rationalisation of the normative aspect of world views. Only on this level could the social world be conceived of as the totality of 'legitimately regulated interpersonal relations'. The individual had to feel that he or she *had the right* to act in a purely goal-oriented fashion, within certain legal limits, and could at this stage of moral consciousness 'ideally' only feel so when law was seen, not as divinely inspired or traditionally given, but as the free creation of, in principle, free and equal people who could, in freedom, decide which norms should attain, retain or lose validity. This does not mean that Habermas pleads for the basic identity of 'morality' and 'legality'. He does recognise that modern law operates with an idea of legality which has little to do with morality, but he stresses, at the same time, that it can only do so because the body of law *as a whole* is conceived of as having a moral basis. The necessity for the moral foundation of law has been shifted, and therefore *apparently* removed, for large areas of the law, but it has not been eliminated. This does not imply that the basic legal institutions, which render legitimacy to the body of law as a whole, such as a modern constitution, cannot be criticised for the way they are sometimes tied up to particular interests, say certain class interests, rather than general interests. But this criticism can only have a basis exactly when it is presupposed that there *should be* this moral basis for modern law.

Habermas' third point in the illustration of his view that Weber totally lost sight of the possibility that rationalisation in law could have a value-rational basis is certainly not the least important one. It has to do with an essential element in Weber's analysis of this process, namely his picture of the dialectic of formal and substantive rationality in law. What do these terms stand for? The formal rationality of law was, for Weber, a matter of the endeavour to find the juridically most precise form, and the most adequate one for the calculation of chances and the systematisation of law and legal procedure. Substantive rationality, however, had to do with the attempt to transform law in such a fashion that it could best satisfy the ethical and practical-utilitarian requirements of those who used it (cf. Weber, 1922:467).

Habermas believes that Weber's interpretation of the demand for substantive rationality as mainly a disturbance of its formal rationality, and therefore as basically irrational, again provides evidence for the fact that the latter really identified rationality with goalrationality.

Finally, we have indicated in the first part of this book that Habermas himself sees law as instrumental in the disjunction of subsystems of goalrational action from their moral-practical basis. He coins the term juridification for this phenomenon. We remind the reader of this to avoid the impression that Habermas, in his polemics against Weber, pictures the rationalisation of law as exclusively a matter of value rationality. This is certainly not the case. 'But this growing autonomy of self-regulated subsystems in relation to the communicatively structured lifeworld', says Habermas, 'has less to do with the rationalization of action orientations than with a new level of system differentiation.' This too could not be grasped by Weber within the restrictions of his action theory. It is considerations such as these which have induced Habermas to transform the action-theoretical approach through the theory of communicative action and to link action theory with systems theory (cf. Habermas, 1984a:I 270–71).

We have endeavoured in this book to make a clear separation between the exposition of Habermas' views and critical comment on them. An overview of critical comments on Habermas can be found in the last chapter. We have therefore so far refrained from posing the question whether Habermas' interpretations of the classics are correct. The fact that we are now going to ask this very question as far as Weber is concerned should not be seen as an inconsistency. This also is for reasons of exposition, not of the views of Weber but rather those of Habermas. We believe that Habermas' interpretation of Weber's views on the rationalisation of law is rather one-sided and that this one-sidedness has a great deal to do with Habermas' long-established notions on the nature of different types of knowledge and the cognitive interests which lead to their accumulation.

What we will particularly criticise in Habermas' interpretation is his claim that Weber virtually equated the rationality of law with goalrationality and that his rather negative views on attempts to introduce elements of substantive rationality into law should be explained from this equation.

Before we go any further into this claim we should state here categorically that Weber did not equate formal and substantive rationality with, respectively, goal- and value rationality. It is clear that formal rationality is not the same as an ends-means rationality unless it is conceded that here the goal is set *within* the law, namely in the form of an 'immanent' requirement for its logical consistency and what Weber called 'deductive stringency'. This doesn't of course imply that formally rational law cannot be used in a goalrational fashion. In fact its precision and systematisation make it eminently suitable for the calculation of the chances of those to whom the law is applied. Weber has pointed out repeatedly that such calculability is an important element in economic and bureaucratic rationalisation. We remarked too that substantive rationality is not to be identified with value rationality. Weber did not regard substantive rationalisation as a matter of the system-atisation of law on the basis of general ethical principles. The principles substantive rational law drew on did not have to be of an ethical nature; they could, for instance, also be the clearly formu-lated strategy of certain power politics.

What Habermas has virtually disregarded is that the formal rationalisation of law is to Weber largely a matter of its 'deductive stringency', that is to say its internal logic as a basis for its systematisation. Therefore the formal rationality of law could be eminently non-utilitarian because purely juridical logic often led to results which were deeply disappointing to those who had turned to the law for the solution of some concrete problem or other. Juridical logic was conducive to the idea that what the professional jurist could not conceive of on the basis of the law's general principles did not in fact exist. Those who had an 'external' interest in the administration of law were, however, oriented to its economic utilitarian significance. From the legal-logical point of view this economic utilitarian significance was irrational. Weber gave the example that, according to legal logic, basing itself on the traditional concept of theft, the theft of electricity could not exist. Matters such as these, said Weber, were not the consequence of some special juridical foolishness but rather of the discrepancy between the immanent logic of formal legal thought and the economic utilitarian orientation of those who wanted the law to be administered for some external goal (Weber, 1922:505).

The fact that in Weber's view formal rationality could be far removed from any utilitarian considerations, and thus from goal-rationality, comes out particularly strongly in his comparison of law with music:

> In the case of music, the tension between expressive or pragmatic (e.g., cultic) musical rationality on the one hand and 'pure' rationality devoted to perfecting tone systems and *techniques* on the other; in the case of law, the tension between 'material' rationalization emerging from legal interests and corresponding to extant ideas of justice on the one hand, and a 'formally' rational perfection based on traditions in thought and the needs of legal specialists on the other. (Weber, quoted in Treiber, 1985:844)

(We should point out that the term 'material' rationalisation in this statement stands for what we have called 'substantive' rationalisation.)

Habermas is, of course, not unacquainted with Weber's view of formal rationality as mainly a matter of the internal logic and deductive stringency of law (in fact, he quotes the relevant statements himself), but he disregards it and on occasion argues against it. 'This formal structuring of the law, the unrestricted application of formal-operational thought to the professional practical knowledge of legal specialists, is certainly an interesting state of affairs', says Habermas. 'But the fact that this tendency appears very unevenly in the legal developments of different nations (more pronouncedly in countries within a tradition of Roman law), makes one sceptical regarding any proposal to look for the growth of rationality in modern law primarily in its internal systematization.' (1984:I 256).

Habermas does not elaborate on this argument and thus we have

to demonstrate its revealing character by elaborating on it ourselves. What he seems to be saying here is this: the internal
systematisation of law has progressed more in countries with a
Roman law tradition (e.g. France, Germany, the Low Countries
etc.) than in those without this tradition (the most conspicuous
example of which is England); *therefore* the law's internal systematisation cannot be a criterion for the extent of its rationalisation. This
implicit 'therefore' is interesting because it only makes sense if it is
absurd to believe that the rationalisation of law has progressed less
in England than in the other countries mentioned. But it is only absurd to believe this when the rationality of law is found, in the first
place, in its instrumental applicability, in other words in its
goalrationality. Because England knew capitalist development
earlier than any of the continental countries (this is the implicit
argument) law cannot have been rationalised to a lesser degree there
because the rationality of law is a matter of the goalrationality of its
orientation to, and usefulness for, economic and bureaucratic goals.
So here we come to the interesting result that Habermas' argument
against Weber only makes sense if the rationalisation of law is seen
as a matter of its goalrationality, but this is the very notion
Habermas reproaches Weber for.

As a scholar deeply versed in the history of law, Weber was of
course very well aware of the different paths of the law's development in England and on the Continent, but to him this was precisely
an argument for the view that the formal rationalisation of law had
little to do with its economic utility (cf. Weber, 1922:509–510).
This, however, did not imply that formally rationalised law could
not be of use to the economy. Formal rationalisation could, because
of its character of logical stringency, enhance the calculability
required by a modern economy; in England such calculability was
ensured by the continuity of historical precedent (Treiber,
1985:849).

We raised the problem of whether Habermas' interpretation of
Weber's views on the rationalisation of law was correct because it
seemed to offer the opportunity to reveal some of Habermas' basic
ideas through the effect they seem to have on his interpretation of
others. We have argued that Habermas' assertion that Weber
virtually identified the formal rationalisation of law with an
increase in its goalrationality is definitely one-sided. We have,
however, not yet indicated where in Habermas' ideas the source for
this misinterpretation can be found. We cannot answer this

question at great length here, but want to refer to the short sketch of Habermas' ideas on the different forms of knowledge and the 'cognition-guiding' interests which led to their accumulation which we gave in Chapter 1. It is unclear to what extent Habermas still adheres to these views, but we believe that they were at the basis of his interpretation of Weber's views on the rationalisation of law. Within the context of Habermas' early views on the relation between interests and ideas it is well-nigh impossible to conceive of the rationalisation of a field of knowledge, as Weber did in this case, as a matter of immanent development, the systematic unfolding, through human agents, of the internal logic of that field (cf. Brand, 1977).

Habermas' picture of Weber's alleged view that the incursions of substantive rationality in law led to an infringement of the law's formal rationality and therefore to its rationality as such also needs correction. This interpretation too is based on the view that there is a virtual identification in Weber's thought between formal rationality, goalrationality, and rationality as such. Yet it is interesting to observe that Weber's negative reaction to the intrusion of substantive considerations into the law seems to be based on the appreciation of the law's role in the preservation of certain values rather than that of its goalrationality. This comes out particularly strongly in his review of a now-forgotten book on the labour contract. Weber pointed out there that if German courts were going to deal with issues such as the basic wage on the basis of social-ethical considerations they would switch to a sort of 'Khadi justice'. Courts would in this way be dragged into the class struggle. Their composition and political colour would become an object of the political struggle for power. In isolated instances this could serve the interests of the working class, said Weber, but nothing was more certain, given the social environment of German professional jurists, than that in the long run this would be helpful to people rather removed from the working class (Weber in Baumgarten, 1964:440–41). Substantive rationality, in this view, is only rational for those who happen to strive for the ends which allegedly should determine legal considerations. Formal rationality was, for Weber, based on the useful fiction that it was above anybody's or any group's particular interest. Weber once quoted with obvious approval the great law scholar Jhering who had said of formal justice: 'form is the enemy of arbitrariness, the twin sister of freedom' (quoted in Abramowski, 1966:145 n.82).

It is particularly on this point, of course, that the views of Weber and Habermas sharply diverge. For Weber the claim to substantive rationality is a claim to reasonability, but when this claim is made the question should immediately areise, 'reasonable to whom?' Interests were a matter of values and values were subject to 'value collision'. Weber held, as we saw, that in the process of rationalisation the various 'spheres of life', religion, art, science, the critical sphere etc., became more and more distinctly separated from each other and that at the same time the irreconcilable difference between the various value spheres became apparent. In his last great public speech 'Scholarship as a Vocation' he put it this way:

> If anything, we realise again today that something can be sacred not only in spite of its not being beautiful, but rather because and in so far as it is not beautiful . . . we realise that something can be beautiful, not only in spite of the aspect in which it is not good, but rather in that very aspect . . . It is commonplace to observe that something may be true although it is not beautiful and not holy and not good. Indeed it may be true in precisely these aspects . . . the ultimate possible attitudes toward life are irreconcilable, and hence their struggle can never be brought to a final conclusion. (Weber in Gerth & Mills, 1957:148, 152)

Therefore making choices was inevitable; the reasoning came after, namely in the analysis of the implications of what one had chosen.

Habermas too conceives of rationalisation as an increasingly clearer separation of different 'spheres', but with him this also includes the differentiation of the three formal world concepts to which the various validity claims refer: the world of objective reality (referred to by claims to truth), the world of values and social norms (referred to by claims to rightness) and the world of inner states and feeling (referred to by claims to sincerity or authenticity). According to Habermas it is not so that only the claims to truth, referring to the world of objective reality, can be provided with a foundation through argument. The claims referring to all three of these worlds can be dealt with in argument which, though it refers to different things, has basically the same form. Habermas speaks in this context of the 'procedural unity of reason' and rejects Weber's notions on value collision. It is this 'procedural unity of reason' which constitutes the cornerstone of what he calls a discourse-ethics. The basic principle of this ethics is that only those norms can claim validity which can be acknowledged as valid by all those concerned in the process of participating in a practical discourse. The 'rule of argument' for this practical discourse is that, if norms are valid, the results and side effects which would issue from a general following of the norm for the satisfaction of the interests of each individual involved can be accepted by all without compulsion.

Thus Habermas rejects Weber's notion that value collision is also a matter of irreconcilable validity claims. 'The unity of rationality in the multiplicity of value spheres rationalized according to their inner logics is secured precisely at the formal level of the argumentative redemption of validity claims' (Habermas, 1984a:I 249). Habermas believes that Weber did not distinguish sufficiently between the particular value contents of cultural traditions and the validity aspects under which questions of truth, justice and taste can be arranged and approached rationally. To demonstrate that Weber did not make this distinction Habermas refers to the fact that, in the same public speech quoted above, Weber gave the difference between the value of French and German culture as one example of value collision which could not be scientifically solved (Habermas 1984a:I 250). It could be that Habermas is making things a bit too easy for himself here (Weber could very well have thought here of the formal values under which some of the leading ideas in these cultures could be subsumed), but it seems to be a fact that Weber had a negative attitude, as his friend Heinrich Rickert complained, to philosophical attempts to create 'theoretical clarity' about values and goods and to establish a hierarchy among values.

> If Weber had admitted that these things could be done by disciplined reflection he would, implicitly, have agreed that ultimately science would be able to prescribe for man. A firm indication, through 'scientific' philosophy, of a hierarchy of values would leave to man merely the working out of the casuistry of his moral behaviour. But freedom, in the sense of a personal responsibility for a choice, would then disappear. Weber clung to the idea of the collision of ultimate values, and therefore the impossibility of indicating an absolute hierarchy among them, because he clung to the idea of freedom. (Brand, 1987:67)

Habermas calls this kind of ethical stance 'decisionism' and sees in it only the gateway to irrationality.

Habermas has argued in his comments on Weber's views on rationalisation in religion and law that it was the latter's restrictive notion of action which induced him to overlook other than goalrational developments. He has also argued that that aspect of the 'colonisation of the Lifeworld' which he calls juridification cannot even be grasped within the context of a theory of action, including his own. This development can only be analysed within the context of systems theory. It is the combination of action and systems theory which will allow us to come to grips with the phenomena which Weber signalled, but analysed inadequately (according to Habermas), in his theory of rationalisation.

This combination of action and systems theory has, thus far, been conspicuously lacking in sociological theory. We do, however, have a famous example of a theorist who originally focused on action and action theory to construct, ultimately, a theory of systems in which action was lost from sight. We are referring, of course, to Talcot Parsons. Let us see what Habermas has to say of his work in order to gain a closer understanding of the German theorist's views on the nature of the System.

10
Parsons and systems theory

With many it will have caused some surprise that Habermas deals so very extensively with Parsons in his *Theory of Communicative Action* (in the German version of the book the chapters specifically devoted to Weber and Parsons have an approximately equal size). Parsons' reputation has been in decline over the last few decades. His analysis of society in terms of self-stabilising systems was castigated, notably by 'conflict theorists' and those whose theories are generally classified as interactionism. Also, more recent systems theorists such as Luhmann and Buckley have, in a critical elaboration on Parsons, tried to develop their own conceptual scheme. Parsons' implicit claim to have combined successfully systems and action theory has been taken seriously in some very isolated instances—that of Richard Munch for instance. Münch has made Parsons' theory the basis for sophisticated conceptual elaborations.

Yet Habermas nowadays speaks of Parsons—this has not always been the case—in a tone of appreciation and respect. He judges his work to be unequalled, as far as its level of abstraction, systematic character, scope and inclusion of various research results is concerned, and believes that today no theory of society can be taken seriously which does not take that of Parsons into account.

Very much the same qualifications could be used for Habermas' own work in which, as in that of Parsons, the whole field of sociological theory is drawn on, in an eclectic but systematic fashion, to construct an all-inclusive theoretical framework. It seems clear that Habermas has learned a lot from Parsons, though the qualification 'a leftist Parsons' which one author used for him seems somewhat exaggerated. It is, however, especially the American theorist's inadequacies which have helped his younger German colleague to outline his own main contributions to sociological theory. Habermas states explicitly that in his own theory he has taken his point of departure from the problem of the interrelation between the paradigm action/Lifeworld on the one hand, and the System paradigm on the other. This problem, he says, only comes to the fore with Parsons.

In the first period of his scholarly activity Parsons concentrated on action theory. He then tried to explain the existence of social order by reference to an overarching cultural sphere, which was, among other things, a source of values. In Habermas' view Parsons did not, at that stage of his career, really manage to clarify the relation between this cultural sphere and actual interaction. In his later period Parsons tried to explain the existence of social order via a theory of self-balancing systems, but this theory excluded the existence, and therefore the proper analysis, of such social patho-logies as have in the course of the history of social thought been indicated by various names (Marx's alienation, Durkheim's anomie, Weber's 'iron cage' etc.).

Habermas believes that the cause of these deficiencies was always the same: Parsons had no appropriate idea of communicative action and the complementary concept of the Lifeworld. For various reasons he did not draw on modern analytical philosophy, the philosophy of language, which enabled Habermas to develop these concepts. Let us have a closer look at this.

In Parsons' first period, which is marked by the appearance in 1937 of *The Structure of Social Action*, he opted for (meaningful) social action as a basic social concept; this was in reaction to the strong tendency towards behaviourism in American social thought. But Parsons conceived of social action, in the Weberian way, as goal-oriented action. The actor, who had a goal, was placed in a situation which, from his perspective, consisted of means and conditions.

How could social order exist when we had a multitude of actors with possibly different goals? Parsons attempted to answer this question, says Habermas, in terms of the two modes of action orientation which Weber distinguished, namely goal orientation and value orientation. Thus the social order was maintained via the complementarity of specific interests and through value consensus. Values and interests were, according to the American theorist, integrated by institutions. The two mechanisms which allegedly ensured social order were institutionalisation and the internalis-ation of normative elements. In Parsons' conception normative standards could have, as they had with Weber, the status of ultimate and independent goals. The actor's action, which came about in orientation to one of these goals, therefore had the character of 'value realisation'. Since ultimate goals could be entirely different, and even collide, Weber saw 'struggle' (*Kampf*) as one of the basic categories of social life. But Parsons was interested in explaining how this 'value realisation' by monadic actors could yet go together with the existence of a social order. This problem kept pursuing him. Ultimately it would induce him to overlook the monadic actor altogether and to analyse social life in terms of self-balancing systems which yet somehow remained tied up to 'value realisation'. Habermas is convinced that Parsons had to miss the solution of this problem because of his basic mistake in the conception of social action. Social action, as we have repeatedly brought out above, is to Habermas not the affair of monadic actors trying to bring about their own independent goals and somehow creating order in the process. It is rather a matter of actors attempting, via linguistic means, to reach consensus, against the background of a shared Lifeworld. It is on the basis of this consensus that action is coordinated.

It is worth noting that to Weber this conception of communicative action would not have invalidated the notion of 'value collision'—the idea that the irreconcilability of certain ultimate values cannot be brought undone by any amount of discussion and negotiation. Habermas does not accept this because to him values have no transcendental status, they are not placed in a Platonic realm of ideas. The idea of 'rightness' is ultimately a matter of people *agreeing* whether a thing is right. Values are man-made products. Thus they cannot be *inherently* irreconcilable. In Habermas' view, however, Parsons remained on this point a neo-Kantian. He believed to the end in the existence of a transcendental realm of values which he came to call 'the telic realm'. But it was difficult to combine this view with that other Parsonian notion, namely that the social order is a matter of self-balancing systems. In this conception the neo-Kantian notion that transcendental values can only be transformed into entities in the realm of being by the conscious attempts of agents ('value realisation') was bound to disappear from sight.

But before we give more details of Habermas' interpretation of the American theorist's final stage, let us have a closer look at the latter's middle period.

At this stage Parsons analysed society in terms of culture, society and personality, among which three components culture is predominant. We saw above that in Parsons' first stage one of his main problems was how to explain the existence of a social order when he posited at the same time the existence of social actors, orienting themselves to ultimate values, whose value orientation could be quite different. In his middle period Parsons attempted to solve this problem by bringing values nearer to earth as it were. They were located in a culture which is an intersubjective possession. Habermas points out that in this conception social systems and personality systems were seen as two complementary channels through which cultural values were transformed into motivated action. In Parsons' definition (quoted by Habermas) 'social systems are systems of motivated action organized about the relations of actors to each other: personalities are systems of motivated action organized about the living organism' (Habermas, 1987:II 215–16).

What remains unclear to Habermas, in this part of Parsons' work, is how exactly culture can have the integrating role the latter ascribes to it. The actor is conceived of as somehow orienting himself to cultural objects, apparently in very much the same way as he orients himself to objects individualised in space and time. But the cultural objects Parsons was talking about were symbolically embodied meanings which could, in Habermas' view, only be generated or made accessible in (at least virtual) participation in communication processes. This problem was not solved by Parsons' recognition of the existence, beside those cultural objects of orientation, of elements of culture which were internalised (need-dispositions) or institutionalised (role expectations).

Since Parsons lacked the conception of a Lifeworld, and of communicative action which maintains and perpetuates this Lifeworld in the very process of being sustained by it, he could not really explain how culture, society and personality were interlinked. The action orientation Parsons spoke of seemed to retain a random character. He remained unable to indicate the link between culture and action because he had no proper notion of the nature of the 'transmission belt' between these, namely the interpretive, consensus-seeking activities of actors.

This basic flaw was, in Habermas' view, not rectified by Parsons' attempt to bridge the gap between culture and action by the introduction of the 'pattern variables'. These variables indicated the polar alternatives which, allegedly, the actor was faced with in each action situation. Cultural values influenced the choice between these alternatives. Though this is not a treatise on Parsons it might be useful to refresh the reader's memory on this point. The polar variables between which actors, according to Parsons, had to choose were the following: universalism/particularism, performance/quality, (affective) neutrality/affectivity and diffuseness/specificity. We can clarify these terms with a few examples, partly provided by Parsons himself.

Let us take the polar opposition between universalism and particularism. When a person chooses a physician on the basis of this person's supposed technical competence the criterion for the choice is universalistic. When however the choice is made because the physician happens to be the brother-in-law of a personal friend the criterion is particularistic.

Parsons also provides some good examples to highlight the distinction between diffuseness and specificity. The relationship between a physician and a patient is (generally) specific, that between spouses diffuse. When a physician wants information about a patient's private life his query is justified by his specific function of caring for his patient's health. But, says Parsons, 'the basis of a wife's claim to a truthful answer to the question "What were you doing last night that kept you out till three in the morning?" is the generally diffuse obligation of loyalty in the marriage relationship' (Parsons, 1967:360).

The distinction between performance and quality has to do with the difference between the judgment of a physical or social object on the basis of 'what it does, achieves or effects' and that based on the importance attributed to the object itself 'independently of its achievement or its benefit to the actor' (Rocher, 1974:38). One can highlight this difference by comparing the action of a man who decides to keep a dog because it is good at keeping strangers at a respectful distance with the decision of someone who decides to put up with an aging dog because it is lovable.

Finally, the terms affective neutrality and affectivity are almost self-elucidatory. An instrumental relationship, which does not exist for its own sake but for that of some external goal or other, for instance the relation between employer and employee, is characterised by affective neutrality. Affectivity can be found in kinship relations or friendship.

Habermas notes, as many others have done, that the selection of these pattern variables remained arbitrary and that they owed such plausibility as they had to the fact that they seemed to cover the transition from 'community' to 'society', in Tönnies' terms. Parsons could then analyse rationalisation as the progressive institutionalisation of value orientations, which guaranteed certain choices among the alternatives (namely those on the 'society' side of the continuum).

Apart from this objection Habermas has one more weighty within the context of this exposition of his own views. He notes that Parsons presented the pattern variables as the common structural core of culture, society and personality. But if this is so how can we explain the differences in the specific influence each of these elements has on action orientation? Thus this model does not allow us to analyse how actors build up common action orientations from the different resources of the Lifeworld, such as 'acquired competences, acknowledged norms and transmitted cultural knowledge . . .', that is, the very things indicated by Parsons with the terms personality, society and culture. The American theorist did not focus on actors' interpretive activities in which these resources were drawn on, at the same time as they were kept together. Thus he could not explain how society, culture and personality remained interconnected. '*Without the brackets of a lifeworld centered on communicative action, culture, society, and personality fall apart*', says Habermas (1987:II 225). Instead of operating with the equivalent of a Lifeworld concept, Parsons came to conceive of culture, society and personality as three analytically separate systems which mutually penetrated each other. The action-theoretical perspective was now definitely left behind.

In this period Parsons' theory was still clearly displaying the hybrid character it owed to the fact that culture, and the values it harboured, was recognised as a system but at the same time as something quite different. The leading idea with systems, such as the social system and the personality system, was that they had to maintain their boundaries in an environment which could only be partially controlled; their elements were kept together by this functional imperative for boundary maintenance. The elements of culture, however, though it was equally called a system, had according to Parsons 'logical or meaningful rather than functional relationships with one another'. Accordingly, at this stage he made a distinction between functional and social integration: the latter involved the maintenance and integration of cultural values incorporated in the action system.

There was, however, in his view an enduring conflict between the imperatives for culture, namely the requirements of consistency, and functional imperatives. Successful adaptations of the social and personality system to a changing environment could be at odds with prevailing cultural standards. Though Parsons depicted this type of situation as a source of change, or pathological symptoms in action systems, according to Habermas he did not really have the theoretical means to analyse cultural resistance against functional imperatives. How did a culture which in the neo-Kantian view transcended society and personality operate on these or resist the imperatives emanating from them? In Habermas' view only the notion of communicative action which, in reproducing the symbolic structure of the Lifeworld always involves validity claims referring to norms and values, and thus is bound to reflect the 'logic' of the cultural sphere, can explain the resistance of the latter against System imperatives.

Habermas *does* agree with Parsons' distinction between social integration, which is to Habermas part of the symbolic reproduction of the Lifeworld, and functional integration. Social integration has to do with the actual action orientation of actors, and the coordination of these; functional integration is a matter of the 'interwovenness' of action consequences which remain latent, that is they go beyond the 'orientation horizon' of participants. Habermas' proposal to understand societies as the 'systemically stabilized complexes of action of socially integrated groups' contains both these aspects. Thus the material reproduction of the Lifeworld should not be understood as the intended result of cooperation (Habermas, 1987:II 201, 233). However, in Parson's last phase the distinction between social and functional integration disappeared as well. Let us have a closer look at this.

In this last phase Parsons introduced the concept 'action system', as a special case of living, boundary-maintaining systems, to indicate society. The action system had, from an analytical point of view, the following four subsystems: the cultural, the social and the personality systems, and the behavioural organism. Each of these was specialised in a different function: the cultural system in that of pattern maintenance, the social system in the integration of acting units, the personality system in goal attainment, and the behavioural organism in adaptation. We said above that these distinctions were meant to be analytical. Parsons maintained that in actual fact every empirical system consisted of all of these subsystems at once: ' . . . there is no concrete human individual who is not an organism, a personality, a member of a social system, and a participant in a cultural system' (Parsons quoted in Habermas, 1987:II 235). Yet, as Habermas points out, in his actual treatment of these distinctions, Parsons was inclined to see them as real, concrete entities. The actual action unit was regarded by him as created in processes of exchange of the various components of the action system, namely the subsystems which we distinguished above. These subsystems were seen as having relative independence, especially the cultural system, which allegedly followed its own imperatives of pattern maintenance. The subsystems could be placed in a control hierarchy with, from top to bottom, the cultural, social and personality system, and the behavioural organism. The top ones were relatively high in information, the lower ones relatively high in energy.

In this new perspecive the distinction between social and functional integration disappeared. Parsons no longer looked at the social system from the vantage point of the agent, but at the individual agent from the vantage point of the System. Systemic problems, the problems of maintaining systemic balance, were allegedly transformed in action orientations via the pattern variables.

We saw that, at an earlier stage, the relation between values and social systems and personalities was, in the style of Weber, regarded as a matter of value realisation. Now, as we saw above, Parsons spoke of a hierarchy of systems with information flowing from the top (the cultural system) to the bottom.

In Habermas' view Parsons was still trying, but in vain, to incorporate his neo-Kantian heritage into his systems theory. There remained a 'secret idealism' in his views according to which the relations of personalities and social systems with 'non-empirical reality' were mediated through the cultural system.

In his last stage Parsons called the transcendental, non-empirical sphere the 'telic system', which stood, allegedly, in 'cybernetic superordination' to the action system. Habermas sees here merely an 'unjustified duplication of the cultural component of the action system'. This is as far as the—according to Habermas—flawed compromise goes between Parsons' neo-Kantian theory of culture and his systems theory (Habermas, 1987:II 251–56). A more important matter in our context (more important because Habermas' own views can, here again, be effectively highlighted by comparing them with those of Parsons) is that of the reduction of social to system integration.

Parsons saw, on this point, no *basic* difference between coordination achieved by language and that acquired by, for instance, money. Habermas, of course, strongly opposes this view. We are by now familiar with his opinion that only material reproduction can take place via non-linguistic steering media, and that the symbolic structure of the Lifeworld remains a matter of communicative action.

We saw above that, with the process of rationalisation of the Lifeworld, its totally undisputed area, on which actors can draw in communicative action, becomes smaller and smaller. Accordingly, the burden of integration and the risk of misunderstanding increase. Parsons and Habermas are in agreement that a non-linguistic steering medium such as money can provide a relief mechanism in this situation. Parsons claimed that it freed people 'from the efforts to negotiate basics all the time' (Parsons, quoted in Habermas, 1987:II 262).

There remains, however, a strong difference, says Habermas, between, on the one hand, communicative action, in which ego must induce alter to accept validity claims by reasons, and, on the other, result-oriented (strategic) action in which the possibilities for alter are schematised and he is empirically, rather than rationally, motivated. Alter's schematised possibilities, when the coordination of action is reached on the basis of empirical motivation, are, in the case of money, buying or not buying, and in the case of power, compliance or non-compliance.

A steering medium cannot provide a relief mechanism when somehow it causes new burdens of interpretation and increases the risks that consensus will not come about. On this score there is already a considerable difference between money and power. Power is less measurable than money; there is a plurality of power symbols, from uniforms to official seals. Power cannot circulate as freely as money. Above all, power needs legitimation. Money is used in exchange in which, in principle, neither party is damaged. This is not the case with power, the use of which is based on the possibility of *damaging* the other party in case of non-compliance. This possibility has to be made acceptable by the idea that power is used for collectively desired goals. Ideas on the question what then is a matter of common desires either need to be based on traditional consensus or have to be defined in communicative processes oriented to shared understanding. Power is thus tied up to a consensus reached by linguistic means.

This holds, a fortiori, for the other steering media proposed by Parsons, such as influence and value commitment. Not only is it even less possible to measure, alienate and store these than power, what is decisive here is that they remain, ultimately, dependent on linguistic consensus formation. These steering media, as we saw above, 'condense' linguistic means for reaching shared understanding but do not replace them. Validity claims put forward by the man or woman with influence will be less prone to immediate scrutiny. The 'warrants' for it are not immediately found in 'good reasons' but rather in the background of culture and socialisation. But influence itself remains, even more than power, tied up to linguistic consensus formation.

Parsons' failure to distinguish the System from the Lifeworld, and thus social from functional integration, makes him unable to analyse properly the 'social pathology' of the modern era. Parsons disagreed with Weber's view that modern moral consciousness, based on principles, could have no chance to develop unless it was embedded in a religious world view. Habermas shares this disagreement but points out that the loss of meaning and loss of freedom, which Weber saw as possible consequences of rationalisation, were not figments of the latter's imagination but real phenomena. Parsons identified the rationalisation of the Lifeworld and the increase in System complexity, and interpreted disturbances of the Lifeworld as fortuitous and temporary disturbances of systemic balance. We can only speak of a systemically induced pathology, says Habermas, when relevant groups experience structural changes as a threat to their identity. Since Parsons had abandoned the concept of social action, and with it the inner perspective of those who participate in it, he could not even signal this type of crisis, let alone analyse it.

We saw above that to Habermas the disjunction of System and Lifeworld is a necessary condition for the transition from the stratified political class societies of European feudalism to the economic class societies of the early modern era. In the process new subsystems come about, in which action coordination takes place via the steering media of money and power. It is the penetration of these into the Lifeworld, with the consequent 'thingification' of its symbolic structures, which Habermas calls the colonisation of the Lifeworld. In our last chapter we will have a closer look at this. Here we also have the appropriate context to discuss Habermas' views on Marx's relevance for a theory of the modern era.

11
Marx and the 'colonisation of the Lifeworld'

We saw earlier that Habermas believes that for the right indication of the causes for the 'colonisation of the Lifeworld' we should go to Marx. Yet he finds a lot to criticise in Marx's approach. So much, in fact, that one wonders why he has called the final chapter of *The Theory of Communicative Action* 'From Parsons via Weber to Marx'. To him this title is apparently justified by his main thesis concerning the cause of the colonisation of the Lifeworld, which refers to the containment, through welfare state measures, of class conflict in the industrial societies of the West. This, says Habermas, 'sets in motion the dynamics of a reification of communicatively structured areas of action, which, while still conditioned by capitalist relations, works itself out in ways that are less and less class-specific' (1987:II 302).

Before we have a closer look at this thesis we will indicate here, as briefly as we can, Habermas' main comments on Marx. He lauds Marx's theoretical strategy found in the double-sided character of his analysis of the 'commodity form'. This analysis enabled Marx to look at the development of capitalist societies both from the System perspective of the observer, as well as the Lifeworld perspective of those potentially involved. From the observer's System perspective society appeared as the steering mechanism of a self-regulating process of reproduction, in which variable capital was exchanged against labour power. From the participants' Lifeworld perspective it appeared as classes. In terms of Habermas' concepts, the imperatives of systematic and social integration coincided in Marx's analysis of labour power. Labour power was expressed in the concrete action of the Lifeworld producer, but it was also an achievement within the functional whole of the capitalistic enterprise and the economic system as such. The transformation of labour power into abstract labour was concomitant with a change in the coordination of interaction, which now no longer took place via norms and values but over the medium of exchange value. Participants in this interaction adopted for themselves, and assumed in others, an objectivating disposition and transformed social and intrapsychic relations into instrumental ones.

To Habermas the strength of Marx's approach is that it allows for the translation of propositions concerning the System (on anonymous value relations) into historical ones (on the interaction between social classes). Problems of system integration can be related to the dynamics of class conflict. For Marx this was a critical approach because it allowed him to denounce the process involved in the upkeep of the economic subsystem as a dynamics of exploitation which was made unrecognisable by reification.

Habermas, however, also finds basic flaws in this approach, because it remained wedded to a philosophy of history in which both System and Lifeworld, though analytically distinguished as far as their mutual relations were concerned, were yet seen as parts of a whole of which the separate elements were destined to disappear. Translated into concrete terms, this philosophy of history allocated to the revolutionary proletariat the role of taking the economic system back into the Lifeworld. This was the famous transition from the 'realm of necessity' into the 'realm of freedom'.

Habermas confronts Marx's view that the abolition of the private ownership of the means of production would lead to the disappearance of capitalism, and the total democratisation of economy and state, with Weber's much more accurate prognosis that the abandonment of private capitalism would in no way bring about the destruction of the iron cage of modern industrial labour. Also, Marx was allegedly blind to the fact that the development of the economic subsystem was not only a matter of the dynamics of exploitation but an evolutionary gain, a matter of increased societal steering capacity. The belief that this system could be taken back within the horizon of the Lifeworld was a matter of romantic nostalgia, which also coloured his concept of 'alienation'. Habermas' main objection to this latter concept is that it is just not analytically distinct enough to serve as an instrument of critical theory. Marx used it to express the idea that in capitalism, life was no longer lived for its own sake but merely served to bring about the externalisation of labour power. But the concept of life remained, in this context, too abstract to serve as a critical standard. What critical theory should, in

Habermas' view, indicate is how the conditions for social integration, that is for integration via communicative action, have been negatively affected in the process which he calls 'colonisation'. It should therefore be able to distinguish between rationalisation on the one hand as a process which involves the *differentiation* of the Lifeworld, and on the other its (ultimate) '*thingification*' under the impact of systemic imperatives. With Marx's concept of 'life', which had overtones of a romanticised past, one simply could not make this distinction.

An even more decisive flaw in Marx's theory was, according to Habermas, that it did not offer the theoretical scope to analyse the submission of the Lifeworld to System imperatives not only by the destructive expansion of the medium of money but also by that of power. In Marx's theory of value there was only attention for the medium of money, for the monetarisation of labour power. Marx did not notice that the conditions for social integration via communicative action were negatively affected by the penetration of money as well as power into the Lifeworld, because, like Weber and Parsons, he did not think in terms of communicative action. Marx' fundamental category, that of labour, and his neglect of the difference between labour and interaction, made him consider action as an instrumental goal-oriented activity from the start. Thus the fact that, through the penetration of power into the Lifeworld, communicative action was increasingly replaced by strategic and instrumental action remained invisible to him.

For all these reasons Marx was not able to analyse the 'colonisation' of the Lifeworld, which is a matter of the exchange between it and the political system. In this exchange new balances are created, which prevent alienated labour and 'neutralised' political participation from leading to class conflict. The state's attempt to neutralise the Lifeworld expressions of crises in the economic system leads to the extension and greater density of formally organised realms of action. The thingification effects of this are non-class-specific. The conflict it engenders where the symbolic structure of the Lifeworld is threatened cannot be called class conflict. Indeed, in Habermas' analysis of what he calls the 'new politics' the idea of labour as a structurating force in these matters has been totally abandoned. We will now have a closer look at this.

The 'colonisation of the Lifeworld' is, from the point of view of the System, not entirely successful. In its pacification of class conflict it induces thingification effects which are non-class-specific and arouses protests which, equally, are not limited to any one particular class (Habermas' 'colonisation' metaphor appears well chosen also from this point of view since resistance in the colony against the metropolis also went beyond any one particular class). It is important to notice that there can be protests at all. For Habermas 'thingification' of the Lifeworld is, in contradistinction to older Marxist theory, not merely a matter of mere reflexes induced by System imperatives. Rather these System imperatives *collide* with communicative structures of a rationalised Lifeworld which has its own logic of development. The protests against 'colonisation' are especially found in what Habermas calls the 'new politics'. The new politics have little to do with institutionalised distribution of material goods and with established parties and associations. The System cannot react to the new politics with the usual compensations because the latter is not concerned with distribution problems but with what Habermas calls a 'grammar of lifeforms', that is with problems of the quality of life, equal rights, individual self-realisation, political participation etc. The conflict line is not between classes in the traditional sense but between those who participate immediately in the production process, and are interested in the defence of the welfare state compromise, and those who are further away from it and more sensitive to and/or more affected by the 'self-destructive consequences of the increase in complexity'. What unites this latter category is the criticism of growth.

The new politics comes about on 'the seam' between System and Lifeworld. It deals with problems of overcomplexity and overburdening of the communicative infrastructure. Problems of overcomplexity are generated by processes for which we are morally accountable, because we technically and/or politically initiate them, but for which we cannot really take responsibility because we cannot oversee their consequences. These processes generate abstractions which are imposed on the Lifeworld, and have to be dealt with within it, but yet go beyond its confines. The second category of problems, those which have to do with an overburdening of the communicative infrastructure of the Lifeworld, comes about through the phenomena of deprivation entailed by a 'culturally impoverished and one-sidedly rationalised everyday praxis'. In reaction to these problems new groupings, often based on ascriptive characteristics such as sex, age, colour, denomination or neighbourhood, try to create new forms of community which should help them in their search for a personal and collective identity.

The common target for these alternative groups is the roles which come into existence through the exchange relations between System and Lifeworld: those of employee and consumer, of the state's clients and (pseudo-participating) citizens. They protest against the thoughtless identification of the rationalisation of the Lifeworld with the increase in complexity of the System.

What, under these circumstances, are the tasks of contemporary critical theory? The Marxist theory of value required the translation of processes within the System into those of the reification of living labour. But for Habermas the capitalist economic system embodies not only a new formation of class relations but also a higher level of system differentiation in its own right. Instead of the 'translation' questions the Marxist theory of value went in for, critical theory should pursue the empirical question how and when the growth of the monetary-bureaucratic complex induces pathological effects in the Lifeworld. In doing this, however, critical theory remains faithful to the Marxist example in the sense that it criticises present-day social reality as well as the contemporary social sciences.

The theory of communicative action as critical theory must, in the first instance, 'reconstruct' the rationality of anthropologically basic structures. This rationality is inherent in the whole set of rules structuring communicative action and, as we saw, analysed by Habermas in terms of concepts developed in the philosophy of language. The competent actor is intuitively conscious of the rules which govern the very reproduction of social life. Therefore, as Bernstein puts it, 'emancipatory critique does not rest upon arbitrary norms which we "choose", rather it is rooted in the very structures of intersubjective communicative competence' (Bernstein, 1985:17).

Thus a critical theory of this nature analyses matters, on the one hand, in terms of a logic of development, which finds its guiding thread in the assumed competences of actors and already achieved levels in the learning process inherent in social and cultural evolution, and which together open up possibilities for the unfolding of certain cognitive structures. On the other hand this critical theory operates with the concept of the dynamics of development, which refers to development as it actually took place under the influence of all kinds of historical events. What has actually come about through the dynamics of development can then be critically compared with what would have been possible on the basis of the logic of development.

Critical theory is, in its form of the theory of communicative action, a theory of rationality. That is why it can be a critical theory in the first place: the concept of rationality is a normative concept. We saw above that the strength of Habermas' critical approach is to be found in the fact that he does not, as Weber and the early Frankfurters did, limit rationality to goalrationality. Therefore goalrational developments in the System can, in principle, be submitted to normative restrictions from the Lifeworld, which owe their development and prestige to the deployment of the whole spectrum of rationality. Habermas thus offers on this point a far more 'optimistic' view than either Weber or the early Frankfurters did. The 'colonisation of the Lifeworld' is not an inevitable state of affairs but rather one based on contingent causes which are in principle open to change through political action.

The normative concept of rationality is not applied to social developments from outside, as it were, but gained in a reconstruction of the basic structure of communicative action and communicative rationality. For Habermas, as we saw above, reason has not merely to do with the truth of utterances but is constituted by 'the unity of theoretical reason with practical-moral insight and aesthetic judgment', which comprehends the cognitive, normative and expressive aspects of rationality. The theory's critical task also implies the inquiry into whether the unity of this rationality can be maintained after a rationalisation process, in which Reason has been dispersed into its various elements. It implies, furthermore, the inquiry into how contact can be established between the expert cultures of today and everyday praxis. It must trace the paths along which science and the humanities, morality and art, which have each developed their own criteria of validity (respectively truth, rightness and authenticity) can still communicate with each other. In doing all this the theory of communicative action must, however, focus on those elements in the conditions for consensus formation which go beyond the spatial and temporal limitations of any particular context. In retaining this focus it will remain a formal enterprise on a high level of abstraction. The facts, says Habermas, 'will reveal as an incurable romantic one who tries to affirmatively spell out utopia in terms of particular examples ...' (Habermas, 1985b:70).

12
Critical comments

In Habermas' voluminous work, *The Theory of Communicative Action* still stands out as his magnum opus. Though the book has appeared comparatively recently, it has attracted a great deal of critical attention. In our exposition of Habermas' views in the preceding chapters, we have carefully refrained from referring to critical comments, but we will in this chapter review some of these criticisms, and Habermas' replies to them. In doing so we will concentrate on the following themes: the link between language and rationality, the nature of communicative action, the soundness of the conceptual distinction between System and Lifeworld and the evolutionary theory tied up to this and finally, the question whether the theory of communicative action can serve as the basis for a genuine critical theory.

We will indicate here, in very summary fashion, the main line of the composite argument. One of the points raised, and it touches directly on the core of Habermas' views, is that rationality is not 'given' with language but is a matter of the will, and that Habermas' ignoring of this fact has led to his neglect of the problem of human agency and motivation. One author identifies the cause for this neglect in Habermas' allegedly erroneous transfer of Piaget's 'genetic structuralism' from the individual to the species. Further, the point is made that if using language does not in itself imply the unfolding of a potential for rationality, the real sociological problem is which social circumstances are conducive to it.

In his answer to these arguments Habermas stresses that as far as rationality is concerned, the possibility of a choice is merely abstract and does only exist from the point of view of the individual agent. This agent, however, belongs to the Lifeworld, and from the perspective of the Lifeworld there is no such choice. It has to be reproduced through communicative action which draws on the possibilities for rationality inherent in language. He reiterates his various arguments for the existence of these possibilities, of which the main one is that all languages make a distinction between what is true and what we hold to be true and that therefore the supposition of a shared objective world is inherent in all linguistic usage. He argues, in addition, that the dialogical roles in discourse offer the possibility for ego and alter to take over each other's perspectives and for the interchange of participant and observer perspectives. Habermas does recognise the validity of the sociological question which circumstances are conducive to rationality, but sees such problems as entirely separate from those of the developmental-logical delimitation of the ranges of variation in the formal properties of rationality structures.

Habermas' point on the necessity of the reproduction of the Lifeworld and the impossibility, from a Lifeworld perspective, of picturing rationality as only a possible choice, has been argued against, mostly implicitly, by those who have made a frontal assault on his whole conceptual framework, by doubting the soundness of the distinction between Lifeworld and System and his allocation of different types of action to these spheres. Habermas' reaction to this has been, on the one hand, to put a considerable amount of water into his wine by denying that he has made the sharp distinctions ascribed to him and, on the other, to maintain that there *are* differently integrated realms of social reality. The steering media of money and power keep the juridically constituted economic and administrative action systems together as a separate realm.

One of the main questions involved here is whether Habermas' alleged partial acceptance of systems theory has blunted the critical edge of critical theory. Other critics again wonder whether this latter phenomenon could not be ascribed to Habermas' allegedly ingrained neo-Kantianism which keeps him wedded to the idea that the world consists of two separate realms, that of thought and being. Therefore he can only conceive of rationality as procedural and his critical thought is devoid of empirical content. Others have attacked the status of theory as critical theory on an even more fundamental level by throwing doubt on Habermas' assumption that understanding (by agents as well as by social scientific interpreters) requires judging. If the theory of society owes its critical status to this basic tenet as, for instance, Herbert Schnädelbach claims, doubts about this also reflect on its assumed critical potential.

This section on the status of critical theory ends by drawing attention to what we regard as one of the main practical difficulties for critical theory in Habermas' conception of it, namely the lack of an adequate criterion for distinguishing between systemic developments which should be regarded as evolutionary gains and those which have to be considered as a nefarious 'colonisation of the Lifeworld'. Let us now have a closer look at the details of these arguments.

One of the main bones of contention between Habermas and his critics is the assertion that there exists a link between language, rationality, and a counterfactually posited ideal speech situation. 'Is not language more aptly regarded, with Wittgenstein, as *all* the things that can be done in and through language?' asks Giddens (1982:335). And the German philosopher Rüdiger Bubner (1981:189) makes a similar point when he protests against the 'equation of language and reason', against what he calls 'the thesis of an "a priori intelligibility" of the emancipatory interest in the medium of language . . .'

Many critics point out that being rational requires a form of commitment, that the mere fact of entering into communication does not imply, in itself, the willingness 'to yield to the better argument'. Agnes Heller (1982:29) makes a distinction between rationality in itself and rationality for itself and emphasises the fact that the latter requires a choice. Habermas' old sparring partner Niklas Luhmann puts it as follows: 'There are too many grounds and arguments . . . When it has not been very precisely determined in advance what is relevant and what is not . . . communication can, in actual fact, not lead to anything' (Luhmann, 1982:372–73).

Following this line of argument one could say that the decision on what is relevant and what is not is not given with language itself but is a matter of the will. That great commentator on the varieties of Marxism, Leszek Kolakowski, also had this point in mind when he wrote that Habermas was, in accordance with 'the whole tradition of German idealism', in search of a focal point 'at which practical and theoretical reason, cognition and will, knowledge of the world and the movement to change it, all become identical'. Kolakowski obviously does not believe that there is such a focal point. In trying to answer the question whether one state of affairs rather than another constitutes emancipation, he says 'we cannot avoid making a decision that goes beyond our knowledge of the world'. There can be no vantage point 'from which the distinction between knowledge and will can be seen as eliminated' (Kolakowski, 1987:III 393).

An American commentator (Dickens, 1983) makes much the same point in a reaction to some distinctions Habermas came up with in reply to critical comments on his earlier works, namely the distinction between discourse and ordinary speech and between reflection and reconstruction and which in the view of this commentator do imply (and should imply for Habermas) 'the separation of knowledge from processes of enlightenment'. But if this is granted one can no longer agree to the claim that there is 'an emancipatory potential in the very structure of language itself'. Dickens quotes here with approval Bernstein's statement that what 'seems to be lacking here is any illumination on the problem of human agency and motivation' (Dickens, 1983:154).

Some critics have seen Habermas' lack of attention to agency as a consequence of his neglect of inner nature, of the reality and independence of the body. Joel Whitebook argues that, though inner nature can be drawn into the 'web of intersubjectivity' by language, it does not follow that inner nature is linguistic in itself. Habermas implicitly denies the existence of the unconscious as a 'non-linguistic substratum' and 'fails to capture the sense of an "inner foreign territory" which is a hallmark of Freudian thought; in principle, everything is potentially transparent. As a result, he is in danger of losing sight of the opposition between reason and the drives altogether' (Whitebook, 1985:157).

Alford sees the origin of Habermas' 'abstract and shadowy view of the individual' in his attempt to 'humanise' Freud, to conceive of psychoanalysis as a 'depth hermeneutics' which interprets psychopathology in terms of the suppression of communication. The phenomena psychoanalysis is concerned with are, in this view, linguistic or at least pre-linguistic in character. Psychopathological symptoms are thus regarded as expressions of a private language which allegedly comes about when traumatic events cause a '*deviation from the model of the language game of communicative action*, in which motives of action and linguistically expressed intentions coincide' (Habermas, quoted in Alford, 1987:12). The fact that drives play no role in Habermas' understanding of the individual has as its consequence that the individual can also no longer be conceived of as a source of opposition to society.

In its place, as a source of opposition to totalitarian socialization by parents and state, Habermas puts language, especially discourse.

> However, it is most problematic whether language can fulfil this function. Even more problematic is whether it should. For language to fulfil this function the individual must be rendered in more abstract and shadowy terms than need be. (Alford, 1987:16)

The way Habermas pictures things it seems as if there is hardly any difference between individual and social needs. In this view only cultural consensus should decide on what individual needs should be fulfilled. Contrary to the suggestion, implicit in Habermas' recognition of a formal world concept having to do with subjective states of feeling, to which the individual has privileged access, Alford argues that, in Habermas' conception of things, 'individuality becomes so thoroughly mediated in language that the individual's access to himself is—ideally—identical with the access of others to him in discourse' (1987:20).

The very idea of being human implies to Habermas the expression of communicative rationality, which is acquired in a collective rather than individual learning process, or rather, in which no real distinction is made between the two. It might well be the case that Habermas' alleged neglect of the individual is primarily due to the model he has chosen for the development of his framework for the history of the species. This model is, as the German scholar Barbara Freitag has convincingly argued, the 'genetic structuralism' he found in Piaget (but which has manifold intellectual roots in authors Habermas has been familiar with from an early stage in his career). Whereas Piaget sees the development of consciousness as a matter of progressive problem solutions by the individual, Habermas conceives in these terms of the development of species competences. In the process he takes over the inbuilt 'optimism' of Piaget's model and applies this to the history of the species. This 'optimism' is, in the case of Piaget's account of the development of individual consciousness, based on the fact that reason, or the potential for it, is reborn with each child; it is also based on the conception of the development of intelligence as a mathematical-cybernetic system, which has self-regulating mechanisms assuring its maintenance and development.

Freitag (1983:570) is severely critical of all this. She feels that Piaget's model of the development of individual consciousness cannot be applied to the species as a whole, if only because this model does not allow for deviant developments and pathologies. For us another point is of greater importance here. If the development of rationality is an affair of the species the distinction between rationality in itself and rationality for itself does, indeed, make no sense. The individual's rationality, as expressed in communicative action, is then tacitly derived from its source in the (increasing) rationality of the species as a whole.

This does, however, not satisfy critics such as Rüdiger Bubner (1981:108) who argues that an individual commitment to rationality cannot be derived from anything else and that rationality does not even coincide with the rules of normal logic. Habermas' use of the concept of the ideal speech situation does not change this at all, according to Bubner. He believes that two points should be made here. First, engagement in rational dialogue requires a decision. The notion that once we engage in dialogue we cannot avoid being guided by the 'counterfactual ideal' of the 'ideal speech situation' does not constitute an argument against the necessity of this decision 'since it already presupposes the very thing which is being questioned ... The question ... was what compels us to decide to undertake a rational dialogue' (1981:8). Bubner makes this point more specifically against Habermas' old comrade in arms, Apel, but it is equally relevant in comment on Habermas' work. The second point to be made here is that (rational) argumentation does not in itself lead to (rational) action. 'One of the oldest, and so far never satisfactorily solved, puzzles of ethics', says Bubner, 'consists precisely in guaranteeing the transfer of correct insight into action' and he states elsewhere that 'the replacement of the guidance of action by the logic of argumentation also expresses the oldest objection to rhetoric' (Bubner, 1981:153, 152). In his contribution to Thompson and Held's anthology of articles on Habermas, Bubner returns to this point. There he makes the claim that the problem of sophistry arises when language, which is merely the means towards knowledge, becomes the one and only end (1982:51).

If the use of language, then, does not in itself imply the unfolding of a potential for rationality, the sociological question to be asked is what social circumstances are conducive to rationality. This is a point made by quite a few critics. Johannes Weiss remarks that the validity claims Habermas often refers to can only impress, motivate and oblige under certain social and institutional constellations and psychic dispositions. Thus an empirical theory of society should aim at the elucidation of these empirical conditions for the development and the obligatory character of rationality. If the idea of Reason is exclusively 'reconstructed' from communicative action and the idea of communicative rationality thus gained is conceived of as the determining force of social change, the levels of logical-philosophical and historical-sociological analysis are shifted too much into each other (Weiss, 1983:113).

Stefan Breuer (1982:144) makes a similar point in a rather hostile article, written from a Marxist point of view. He adds to it the remark that Habermas' reconstruction of social evolution is unacceptable not because it gives a predominant place to mind but because it cannot give a social scientific explanation of this predominant place. It is therefore a philosophy of history in the bad sense of the word. A Dutch commentator, Frans van Doorne (1986:85), believes that Habermas in general does not distinguish with sufficient clarity between two contexts of analysis: the context of formal, universal-pragmatic analysis and the context of empirical research.

We should have a look now at Habermas' reply to some of these points. Let us go back to the criticism that Habermas has wrongly suggested a necessary link between language, rationality, and a counterfactually posited ideal speech situation, and the question whether we should not regard language as all the things that can be done in and through it. Habermas' first reaction to this is that it strikes him 'as not entirely fair' that he is pinned down (as indeed he often is) 'to one rather strongly formulated sentence' from his 1965 inaugural lecture at Frankfurt. The passage concerned is the following: 'The idea of autonomy and responsibility is given to us with the structure of language. With the very first sentence the intention of a common and uncompelled consensus is unequivocally stated' (Habermas, 1970:50). The first point to be made here is that today Habermas does not only talk about the structure of language as such but also about that of communicative action, that is, the expression of the communicative competence for rationality in and through language. This rationality is inherent, as we saw, in the whole set of rules structuring communicative action. Communicative competence is the ability to operate within these rules. This is an ability of the species as such. There is a unity in the plurality of language games, the unity pointed to in an answer to the question 'how a use of language orientated to reaching understanding is possible'.

Communicative competence is the capacity to handle language adequately as a certain tool in the necessary attempt to reach shared understanding. It is because this tool has certain characteristics that the attempt to reach shared understanding is not always doomed to failure. All languages, says Habermas in a recent article, offer the possibility of making a distinction between what is true and what we hold to be true. The supposition of a shared objective world is inherent in all linguistic usage. The dialogical roles in each discourse offer the possibility for ego and alter to take over each other's perspectives and for the interchange of participant and observer perspectives. It is these formal possibilities Habermas has in mind when he talks, in taking a position against such radical, 'ethnocentric' relativists as, for instance, the contemporary philosopher Richard Rorty, of the unity of Reason. He emphasises that in pointing out these 'formal' possibilities of language, he does not imply that we can somehow take up a point of view outside this world and make use of a single ideal language to make 'definitive' statements. Reason is always 'situated' Reason. Validity claims do, at one and the same time, depend on as well as transcend specific contexts (Habermas, 1988:12).

As the years go on Habermas has started to speak more and more cautiously about such concepts as the 'ideal speech situation' or the 'ideal communication community'. The idealising presuppositions of communicative action should not be hypostatised into the ideal of a future situation of definitely reached, universally shared understanding. Neither is the factor of unconditionality, preserved in the discursive concepts of (fallible) truth and morality, an absolute one. Habermas compares the position of embattled Reason, situated between the rival claims of those who espouse radical relativism and those who want to hold on to some concept of truth, in a somewhat mixed metaphor to that of a quivering scale on a sea of contingencies (1988:13). His ultimate argument, when faced with the relativism of Rorty, Lyotard and others, is not unlike the one Popper used against Kuhn: Kuhn's picture of revolutionary science and that of normal science could not both be true. The fact that we can break through a paradigm in revolutionary science implies that we have a greater capacity for reflexive learning than Kuhn's picture of normal science would suggest. Similarly, Habermas quotes approvingly Hilary Putnam's view that if the distinction between what is here and now held to be true and what would be accepted as true under ideal conditions made no sense, we could not explain how we can learn reflexively, that is, improve our own standards of rationality (1988:11). Habermas also argues strongly against those who state that using language does not commit one to rationality, that one neither has the obligation to agree to rational arguments if the results of that agreement might be unpleasant for oneself, nor can ever have the certainty that others will yield to such arguments. The possibility of choice, referred to in such statements, is merely abstract, Habermas maintains, because it exists from the point of view of the individual actor. But the actor belongs to a Lifeworld, and from the perspective of the Lifeworld there is no such choice. The symbolic structures of the Lifeworld can only be reproduced through communicative action which draws on the possibilities of language mentioned above.

The symbolic reproduction of the Lifeworld requires that traditions are carried on, the identity of social groups is reaffirmed and individuals are socialised. All this can take place only through communicative action which embodies communicative rationality. 'Opting for a long-run withdrawal from contexts of action orientated to reaching understanding, and thus from communicatively structured spheres of life, means retreating into the monadic isolation of strategic action: in the long run this is self-destructive' (Habermas, 1982:227).

Of course one could argue here that the point is that the symbolic structure of the Lifeworld is only reproduced very imperfectly and that Habermas systematically exaggerates the degree of rationalisation of the Lifeworld which is in actual fact characterised by a great deal of systematically distorted communication. This latter point has been made by the Dutch philosopher of science Harry Kunneman, who adds to it that he believes that structural violence in and on the Lifeworld mainly comes about because problem solutions in our society tend to originate in the fields of institutionalised science, in which they have to go through what he calls the 'truthfunnel'. In going through this 'funnel' the problems involved are, in fact, transformed. The funnel only lets through those aspects of problems which can be objectivated and reduces their normative, expressive and aesthetic aspects to an irrational, indigestible rest (Kunneman, 1986:279, 10)

Habermas could retort to this, as he has done to other critics, that it is precisely the reactions to the suppression of communicative rationality, 'the reaction of those who are put to flight or roused to resistance by fateful conflicts, who are driven to sickness, to suicide, to crime, or to rebellion and revolutionary struggle', which show that this rationality 'is already embodied in the existing forms of interaction and does not have to be postulated as something that ought to be ...' (Habermas, 1982:227). He employs the term 'causality of fate' here to suggest the 'inevitable' link between the deficiency in communicative rationality and all the negative phenomena he mentions.

There are at least two questions here. One concerns the rationality inherent in a certain type of language use, the other the actual occurrence of this use. Critics such as Luhmann have doubted the second rather than the first. If, however, it is accepted that rationality is inherent in a certain mode of language use, but the actual occurrence of this use, or in any case its frequency, is doubted, the sociological question is, which social circumstances are conducive to rationality? It is in answer to this and related points that Habermas emphasises again what he sees as the correct procedure in critical theory, namely to 'ascertain the rational content of anthropologically deep-seated structures in a transcendentally orientated analysis which is initially unhistorical'. This procedure necessitates a careful separation of problems concerning, respectively, the logic of development and the dynamics of development, and requires 'a clear analytic cut between social evolution and history . . .' Questions concerning the dynamics of development, that is, among others, those processes which Johannes Weiss refers to when he talks about circumstances conducive to rationality, are, says Habermas, not prejudged by a developmental-logical delimitation of the ranges of variation in the formal properties of rationality structures (Habermas, 1982:253–54).

In another reaction to Weiss' objection, Habermas makes a distinction between the formal-pragmatic and the sociological analysis of the Lifeworld. The former points to communicative competence and communicative rationality and makes it clear why social processes remain generally, as a matter of course, 'on this side of the threshold of manifest conflicts'. Sociological analysis of the Lifeworld, however, looks at everyday communicative practice as a product of cultural tradition, social integration and socialisation of individuals, coming about under the compulsion of material reproduction. These factors limit, as determinants of the action situation, the scope for action in a certain way, but also make it possible in the form of resources. These resources require formal-pragmatic analysis. What is, from the sociological point of view, culture, society and personality, is, from the formal-pragmatic point of view, background knowledge, solidarities and competences. It is these resources which allow the flow of the Lifeworld, branching out over speech acts, into communicative action (Habermas, 1986:369–70).

One can see, in Habermas' replies, the extent to which he relies on his concept of the Lifeworld, and its ramifications, to bolster his views on (the necessity of) rationality. However, this concept itself has been under fire. Herber Schnädelbach (1986:29–30) believes that if one deals with the concept of the Lifeworld the way Habermas does, one can only look at the perspective of the participant from that of the observer. He proposes that in introducing the difference between System and Lifeworld Habermas should limit himself to the type difference between goalrational and communicative action. This type difference, Schnädelbach believes, is enough to justify the introduction of a two-layered concept of society. The question of the relation between the perspective of the participant and that of the observer only complicates matters unnecessarily.

However, the suggestion that Habermas should limit himself to the distinction between goalrational and communicative action, in outlining the differences between System and Lifeworld, is hardly welcome to critics such as Johannes Berger who believe that all social systems are integrated at the same time systemically and socially. Berger also criticises Habermas' analysis of contemporary social pathologies. Habermas can, he says, from his perspective, only perceive the contradiction between linguistically produced Lifeworld structures and the increasing complexity of subsystems of goalrational action. But, says Berger, there are also internal contradictions within the System, and those which result from the penetration of Lifeworld orientations into it. Here we can think, for instance, of the democratisation of the workplace (Berger, 1982:360–62).

In his reactions to these criticisms Habermas acknowledges that Berger is on solid ground. The idea of the disjunction of System and Lifeworld should, indeed, not imply that there are no systemically integrative mechanisms in the Lifeworld at all. The primarily socially integrated fields of action in the Lifeworld are neither entirely devoid of power nor of strategic action. Furthermore, it is quite true that, though the colonisation of the Lifeworld takes place under the influence of systemic imperatives, these imperatives are today also limited by Lifeworld principles. Nevertheless, Habermas insists that his picture of the disjunction between Lifeworld and System remains justified. Economic and political relations can in modern society no longer be sufficiently explained from the Lifeworld aspect. Also, the Lifeworld can be negatively defined as the totality of action fields which cannot be described as media-steered subsystems. The idea of the disjunction between System and Lifeworld can, says Habermas, be justified on action-theoretical grounds as well. Normally those who act strategically retain the Lifeworld, even when it no longer has the power of coordination, in the background. But when there is a transformation to media-steered interaction, the acting agent can only retain his or her result-oriented disposition under the condition of an objective reversal of means and ends. The medium itself now transmits the imperatives for retaining the integrity of the subsystem to which it belongs. Therefore Habermas no longer wants to talk of systems of goal-rational action. 'Interactions which are guided by media do not embody instrumental, but functional reason' (Habermas, 1986:387, 391). If one wants to understand what he is driving at here one only has to look at the way in which 'functional reason' has penetrated into much of present-day governmental-political rhetoric which tends to represent the economy as a realm of ends rather than of means; in other words the upkeep and growth of the economy are depicted as self-justifying goals.

Habermas' translator and one of his main commentators, Thomas McCarthy, has criticised the distinction between System and Lifeworld in a more thorough fashion. He looks at it as the basis for three more specific distinctions in Habermas' work, namely that between two methodological perspectives, two mechanisms of integration and two concepts of society.

As far as the distinction between methodological perspectives is concerned, that is, that between the inner perspective of the participant and the external one of the observer, McCarthy remarks that it is too imprecise to be the basis for a distinction between System and Lifeworld. Habermas has himself acknowledged that in any inquiry into social life interpretive procedures have to play a role and that looking at things from the perspective of the observer is part and parcel of the more general forms of analysis of the Lifeworld.

Neither can the distinction between two forms of integration be a basis for that between System and Lifeworld. We recall that Habermas distinguishes here between mechanisms which harmonise the action orientations of participants, and those which stabilise, through the functional intertwining of action consequences, the non-intended interdependencies of actions. McCarthy argues that participants are often more clearly aware of the functional contributions of economic and administrative action to the material reproduction of society than they are of that of communicative action to its symbolic reproduction. Moreover, each stable realm of social interaction will normally show aspects of normative as well as functional integration.

Finally, the distinction between the material and symbolic reproduction of society is equally unable to carry that between System and Lifeworld. Economic and political structures and processes play a part in symbolic, and matters such as socialisation and social integration in material reproduction.

McCarthy also objects to the way in which Habermas has allegedly suggested a pairwise ordering between, on the one hand, material reproduction and goalrational action and, on the other, symbolic reproduction and communicative action. Each concrete field of action can be looked at, he says, from the aspect of goalrational as well as communicative action. Moreover, the systemic perspective directs our attention to aggregated action consequences and that is by no means an immediate function of subjective goal orientation or consciously followed strategies.

McCarthy concludes that Habermas' distinction between System and Lifeworld, and with it his account of social evolution, is deeply problematical. The idea that in the course of evolution new systemic mechanisms come about, which are ultimately detached from the Lifeworld, appears untenable when we observe the facts. Each concrete field of action can be looked at from an action-theoretical as well as a systems-theoretical point of view, can contribute to symbolic as well as material reproduction and requires normative integration, via communicatively shared understanding, as well as functional integration (McCarthy, 1986: 209–211).

McCarthy also has an explanation for what he believes to be Habermas' theoretical misconceptions. In his opinion the German theorist has been seduced by the attractions of systems theory to which, in times gone by, he used to give the cold shoulder. Hence the prominent place of Parsons in *The Theory of Communicative Action*, though this is the same Parsons of whose work Habermas remarked fifteen years earlier that it showed 'a ridiculous disproportion between the piled up mass of empty categorical shells and their meagre empirical content . . .' (quoted in McCarthy, 1986:200). Why does Habermas now want to integrate systems theory into critical theory? McCarthy can see no reason to do so. The doubt concerning the empirical fertility of systems theory, even in its very own field, that of organisation theory, is still very much alive. McCarthy maintains that we do not need systems theory to identify unintended consequences. Equally we do not need it to inquire into the 'functions' which a certain social practice has for other parts of the social whole, because these 'consist simply' of the repetitive effects of that practice on the whole. It might be that systems theory is useful to analyse the inner dynamics of expansive subsystems, such as the economy and the state. The question whether it is useful here is still open but this is, in any case, of little relevance for a critique on Habermas since, in his analysis of the process of the colonisation of the Lifeworld, he takes the expansive dynamics of the System more or less as given. McCarthy asserts that the larger part of what Habermas has to say on 'mediation' by steering media could be stated in action-theoretical concepts (1986:205–7).

The trouble with systems theory, according to McCarthy, is that its arguments are couched in terms of an 'objective purposiveness', of unintentional contributions to the survival of the System. But when can a 'system' be said to survive or have survived? ('Did Germany survive the first World War?') (1986:207). Apart from this theoretical difficulty, McCarthy's main objection to systems theory is that its tendency to define practical-political questions a priori as technical questions implies that it contributes to the depoliticisation of the public sphere and is thus inherently anti-democratic. It cannot, therefore, very well be integrated into critical theory (1986:200). McCarthy believes that Habermas has adopted so much from the conceptual armoury of systems theory that he can no longer answer the question—which certainly is to him too the prime political question of today—which forms of representative democracy and public administration we need. If, in accordance with systems theory, what is social, and therefore potentially an object of the human will, is depicted as only a matter of objectivated relations, questions about the necessary forms of democracy also thoroughly change character (1986:204).

Habermas' reaction to McCarthy's assertions is that he has not made the sharp distinctions and constructed the either-or models the latter ascribes to him. He says that he never wanted to limit functionalism to the phenomena of material reproduction or analyse processes of symbolic and material reproduction only from either the Lifeworld or the System aspect. In principle all phenomena can be regarded from both aspects, though a society can get so differentiated that material reproduction can only be grasped with difficulty from the Lifeworld aspect, and can be better explained from the System aspect. And, conversely, from the point of view of systems analysis one can analyse 'the contributions made by cultural integration, social integration and socialization to the stabilisation of boundaries in an overcomplex environment', but in analysing these with the help of systems theory one has to deal with the limits which symbolical structures impose on steering capacity as contingent data which cannot be adequately explained from this vantage point (Habermas, 1986:381–82).

Habermas does not agree with McCarthy on the explanatory power of action-theoretical concepts, which would allegedly make systems theory a more or less irrelevant intellectual hobby. From the perspective of the Lifeworld, he says, one can hardly explain how aggregated action consequences mutually stabilise in functional relations and generate integrative effects in this fashion. The system-environment model has far more explanatory power here (1986:382).

Habermas denies that he has linked up System and Lifeworld to different action types, namely strategic and communicative action. System integration mechanisms also work through communicative action. Only the steering media money and power require an orientation to strategic action. On the other hand, the Lifeworld is certainly not to be identified with a sphere in which communication is undistorted by power. Thus in most circumstances social integration takes place via a linguistic consensus formation which fulfils the conditions of latent strategic action. Therefore social integration too cannot be identified with any particular type of action.

Here too, however, Habermas emphasises that when we look at the stage of social evolution which is characterised by the disjunction of System and Lifeworld, the terms for particular types of action do not refer merely to aspects but to differently structured realms of social reality (1986:383). This means, of course, that in actual fact Habermas does not accept McCarthy's criticisms wholesale, because the latter certainly did not exclusively speak of premodern societies when he denied the existence of such realms. For Habermas this existence is beyond doubt. With the disjunction of System and Lifeworld, primarily systemically integrated action realms come about. Consensus mechanisms do play a role in their integration but only in an indirect way, namely to the extent that the juridical institutionalisation of the steering media must link up with the normative context of the Lifeworld. We saw above that Habermas is eager to make clear that his disjunction thesis does not imply that system-integrative mechanisms no longer play a role in the Lifeworld. He also acknowledges that his use of words here might have suggested otherwise (1986:387).

We saw too that McCarthy maintained that Habermas' borrowing from systems theory blunted the edge of his critical theory. Habermas points out, however, that the critical potential of his use of systems theory is not limited to the signalling of the reversal of means and ends in media-steered interaction. The really important points here have to do with the structural incompatibility between media-steered interaction and the conditions for the reproduction of the symbolic structure of the Lifeworld. Cultural tradition, social integration and socialisation can only be carried by action oriented to shared understanding, not by power or money. 'Meaning can neither be bought nor compelled' (1986:390).

Habermas' reply to McCarthy does give some credence to Bader's and Giddens' accusation that he tends to use the concepts of System and Lifeworld as referring either to aspects of phenomena or to concrete empirical types. 'First introduced as aspects,' says Bader, 'they are later increasingly and consciously empiricised and understood as concrete spheres' (1986:329). Bader believes that the attempts to achieve an empirical demarcation of these spheres not only remain self-contradictory but that, in addition, they lead to the erroneous picture of the System as monolithic and without inner contradictions. Giddens puts the question point-blank: 'If, as you say, the separation between system and lifeworld is methodological, how can it also operate as a substantive distinction within modernized societies?' (1985:119).

We saw elements of Habermas' answer to these and similar objections above. He has acknowledged that his use of language could lead to reification here, and that he did not mean to suggest that the Lifeworld was totally denuded from system-integrative mechanisms as such, only from the media-steered subsystems. It is the steering media of money and power which keep the economic and administrative action system together as separate realms. These action realms are juridically *constituted* and this is not a matter of just the juridical 'moulding' of a communicative inner structure (Habermas, 1986:386–87). Elsewhere, Habermas has talked of formal organisation as the distinguishing characteristic of these action realms.

These answers will hardly satisfy those who doubt that Habermas made a convincing case for the separate status of System and

Lifeworld. Critics such as Bader (1986:340–41) have argued that the capitalistic mode of production is, as a whole, the opposite of being formally organised. Decisions about allocations in enterprises etc. are taken on the basis of a market situation, and market is the 'classical counter principle to formal organisation'. Apart from this, Bader is also not content with Habermas' statement that formal organisations are characterised by the fact that they are juridically constituted. This, Bader believes, is just a form of legal positivism. Actual social relations in formal organisation are not identical with the relations which have been organised juridically. Nor is it the case that the so-called 'informal relations' in organisations can be regarded as sprouts, as 'tentacles' of the Lifeworld in the System.

Does Habermas' partial acceptance of systems theory make the critical function of critical theory impossible, as both Bader and McCarthy are inclined to maintain? The underlying thought is here obviously that if the steering capacity embodied in the 'functional rationality' of the System is, as Habermas says, to a certain extent an evolutionary gain, but yet the unfolding of 'communicative rationality' today finds its greatest obstacle in this selfsame 'functional rationality', it becomes an impossible task to indicate where exactly this latter form of rationality should be seen as leading to, and where as an obstacle for social evolution. This difficulty is, of course, related to another one, which, as we saw above, Habermas had to acknowledge under the pressure of criticism, namely the fact that it is far from easy to indicate a clearcut demarcation criterion for System and Lifeworld. It can, in view of this, also be seriously doubted whether Habermas' procedural concept of rationality will provide a sufficiently solid basis for critical theory. Its impotence in concrete affairs comes out rather tellingly in the following matter. When Habermas discusses the possibility of criteria on the basis of which we can judge forms of life, he cautiously intimates the possibility that this could perhaps be found in the idea of a balance between factors which need to supplement each other, such as the cognitive, the moral and the aesthetical-expressive (Habermas, 1984ᵃ:I 73). Yet when he was asked point-blank in an interview with the Dutch sociologists Korthals and Kunneman how we should conceive of this balance, he admitted that he had no real idea of this and added that he himself considered this the weakest point in his *The Theory of Communicative Action* (Korthals-Kunneman, 1983: 301–2).

This (self-) criticism does not imply that, with this impossibility of indicating the right balance between the cognitive, the moral and the aesthetical-expressive (and, we may add, that between System and Lifeworld), the whole basis for critical theory has fallen away. We have been merely pointing to some rather conspicuous examples of its critical impotence. Let us now look at the basis of critical theory, as Habermas conceives of it, and comments on this point, particularly those from Helga Gripp.

We saw that the distinction between the logic and the dynamics of development is essential to Habermas' version of critical theory. Allegedly, the theory of communicative action can ascertain the rational content of action structures which are anthropologically given and then developed in the course of evolution. The questions critical theory can ask is which further development of species competences could have taken place, in accordance with the logic of development, and which development has actually taken place, in accordance with the dynamics of development.

Helga Gripp (1984:120) rightly points out that this whole critical enterprise depends on proof that in each communicative action we can, in fact, find the validity claims Habermas distinguishes and that through being equipped with communicative competence we have the capacity for communicative rationality.

Gripp then puts the simple but quite pertinent question why, if we are in principle able to organise our life rationally, we yet obviously don't do this. Habermas could of course answer, she says, that the human species is still at the beginning of its evolution etc., but this same species is able to destroy the world and itself. How can it be that communicative rationality lags so far behind goalrationality? Could it be that language and its immanent rationality structures does not, in fact, have the significance which Habermas supposes it has? And why is it that the three elements of rationality, which we allegedly find in the modern era (the cognitive-instrumental, the moral-practical and the aesthetic-expressive), have no real relation to the rationality of the whole. Where should the explanatory weakness of Habermas' theory be found, asks Gripp?

She is inclined to find this weakness in the fact that Habermas remains, to a certain extent, a Kantian, in the sense that he holds on to the idea that the world consists of two separate realms, that of thought and that of being. Consequently he cannot have recourse to a Hegelian critical procedure, in which historical reality as a particular expression of the absolute mind at a particular stage is confronted with the negation it has to go through on its way to becoming, finally, identical with Mind. Yet Habermas also clings, with Hegel, to the idea that there is a decisive factor in the development of the human species. This is for him, as we saw, the competences of the human species, of which the most important is communicative competence, that is, the capacity for communicative rationality in and through language. However, because Habermas does not want to give up the notion of the split between thought and being he can only conceive of this rationality as procedural, as having to do with the human capacity to determine common goals in discourse, rather than with any empirical content. Gripp believes that it is still very much an open question whether this procedural concept of rationality offers a sufficient basis for an empirical research program of a critical social science (1984:142–47).

One can very much doubt whether Habermas would accept Gripp's characterisation of him as a Kantian. When for instance he comments on Apel's view that in the social reality of the Lifeworld the ideal and the real communicative community are intertwined, he makes a point of saying that this still sounds almost too Kantian and that the 'two-realm theory' has been definitely overcome (Habermas, 1986:367). The reference here is, however, to the realm of values and that of being, which played such a great role in the thought of Rickert and Weber, where the historical agent was seen as situated in an in-between realm connecting the other two realms (that of value and that of being) in its action (cf. Brand, 1987). Whether Habermas could deny that he makes a distinction between thought and being, or would want to deny it, can very much be doubted, though there seems to be an uncertain wavering here which can be particularly noticed in his seesaw between a correspondence and a consensus theory of truth. (Compare here, for instance, his answer to Mary Hesse in Habermas, 1982.) Habermas does not deny that those who look for a guideline to concrete political action in his theory are bound to be disappointed but stresses, on the other hand, that he never had the 'false ambition' to provide this (1982:396).

Is it possible for Habermas, however, to escape from the level of the philosophy of history and to say that the critical dimension of the undertaking of the critical theorist is not basically different from that found in everyday communicative action? The difference between the level of action and that of the interpretation of action only exists for Habermas when the interpreter is dealing with either exclusively teleological or norm-regulated or dramaturgical action. When behaviour is described, however, in terms of communicative action there is no difference between actor and interpreter as far as their potential for interpretation is concerned. Thus those who act and those who theorise about their actions can mutually criticise each other. The social scientist only uses the potential for criticism, to be found in communicative action itself, when he interprets in this fashion, that is as a 'virtual' participant.

This idea can be criticised from several points of view. Bubner tackles the idea of communicative action itself. What is it about? Habermas points to the negotiation of the definition of the situation, on which consensus is reached, as its central element. Bubner takes him, as we already saw above, to task for identifying this with the coordination of action. 'Only that can be coordinated which is already present before the decision to coordinate is taken . . .' In Habermas' view the common definition of the situation seems to absorb both that pre-existent element and the action which is coordinated. The production of a common definition of the situation is identified with the cooperative realisation of action plans. In this fashion one of the main problems of practical philosophy, namely how correct insight is translated into action, is just ignored (Bubner, 1982:352–53).

Other critics again concentrate on Habermas' contention that the interpretation of social action, *Verstehen*, should take place in the performative attitude, and that communicative actions 'always require an interpretation that is rational in approach'. We have already quoted one of Habermas' central statements on this point which avowed that in order to understand an expression, the interpreter must trace the reasons which a speaker could bring up to argue its validity. But reasons cannot, according to Habermas, be described in the attitude of the third person. Their proper understanding requires the performative attitude, the attitude of the participant, and thus the interpreter 'is himself drawn into the process of assessing validity claims'. The obvious question here, of course, is how the sociologist can emerge from the particularism entailed by taking the point of view of the actor. We saw above that according to Habermas this possibility always remained open, to both interpreter and actor alike, because of the rationality inherent in communicative action. This offers 'the critical means to penetrate a given context . . . the means, if need be, to push beyond a de facto established consensus, to revise errors, correct misunderstandings and the like. The same structures that make it possible to reach an understanding also provide for the possibility of a reflexive self-control of this process' (Habermas, 1984a:I 120–21).

Thomas McCarthy does not agree with what he calls this '*very strong thesis*' of Habermas. He believes that interpreters 'raised in pluralistic cultures and schooled in cultural and historical differences are quite capable . . . of understanding symbolic expressions without taking a position on their validity . . .' (McCarthy, 1985:185). McCarthy certainly disagrees with Habermas' view that the interpretation of action requires that the interpreter inquires not only whether an action is in accordance with norms, which are actually regarded as valid in the society concerned, but also whether the norm itself is right. (Habermas has in fact the tendency of regarding the following two statements as necessarily linked in the context of interpretation: 'X follows norm Y rightly' and 'It is right that X follows norm Y'.) McCarthy objects that, though our *capacity* for understanding has to do with our own competence as a social actor and is 'originally acquired in a performative attitude, we do have the ability (also socially acquired) to adopt an objectivating, hypothetical attitude toward the reality so understood, that is, to treat it as an object of scientific inquiry and technical control'. He adds that, of course, '*social facts* do not thereby lose their characteristic differences from purely physical facts' (1985:186).

Schnädelbach enters into the same claims of Habermas by first pointing out their importance. Only if these claims can be validated, together with the claim that communicative action is fundamental to all other types of action, can the theory of communicative action present itself as critical theory. Schnädelbach doubts, however, whether this can be done. Why would the rational interpretation of action, that is, an interpretation from reasons, be the same as interpreting it as rational, he asks (1986:24).

A lot hinges here on the very concept of rationality. Habermas says that if we use the term in relation to changes in the situation of a system or institutional arrangements, which have not come about intentionally, the word is used in a transferred or derived sense. At the background here, according to Schnädelbach, is the debate with Luhmann. Habermas wants to reduce the system rationality of the system theoreticians to system functionality and then make rationality the basis for a critique of functionalist reason. This way of introducing rationality, says Schnädelbach, is related to the thesis of the primacy of communicative rationality over goalrationality. Habermas maintains that the descriptive concept rationality is always also normative. But even if that were the case, says Schnädelbach, and that is by no means clear, the question still remains open whether rationality here has to do with the observer or with the object.

If the latter is the case it only relates to the action orientations of observed persons or social systems and nothing else (Schnädelbach, 1986:19–21). Habermas has tried to abolish this distinction by a universal concept of rationality, a rationality equally shared by the interpreter and the agent who engages in communicative action. But the question has to be asked, says Schnädelbach, whether the alleged genetic and normative primacy of communicative action is extended to the theoretician, who has made of communicative action his theme. If the answer is 'yes' this means that each theoretician participates in his own Lifeworld which is the complement of the one which is thematised. This issues in what Schnädelbach calls a 'universal perspectivism' of the Lifeworld of the interpreter, because he cannot shed the participant's perspective at will. 'Normativism in the sense that the observer always has to take a stand, like a participant, to the validity claims raised in communicative action in order to understand them at all is then assured at the price of relativism' (1986:29).

Habermas answers the points of McCarthy and Schnädelbach in the following fashion. Against McCarthy's view that the interpreter does not have to take a 'yes' or 'no' position and can practise a kind of abstention, he argues that 'abstention' also requires a rationally motivated position which only means that, for the time being, we postpone further interpretive efforts as, for instance, we may do when confronted with a mythical narrative. We will understand this only 'when we can say why the participants had good reasons for their confidence in this type of explanation'. However, to achieve this, says Habermas, 'we have to establish an internal relation between "their" sort of explanation and the kind we accept as correct . . . both modes of explanation have to be located within the same universe of discourse' (Habermas, 1985b:204–5).

Habermas answers Schnädelbach in a similar vein. He comes up with a few interesting examples here in order to illustrate his thesis that to understand is to judge. A mathematical proof, he says, can only be understood to the extent that we can construct it ourselves, which enables us to either accept it as true or to know why it is false.

He says here, as he did to McCarthy, that the interpreter can of course avoid taking a position, but this only means that he has not yet understood what is to be interpreted. Yet Habermas also states that the evaluation of reasons, which takes place in understanding, is not equivalent to taking a 'yes' or 'no' position, as a participant in actual interaction does. The actor commits himself, with the position he takes, to a certain way of continuing the interaction (or breaking it off, as the case may be). The role of the interpreter and the actor, he says here, are of course not identical (Habermas, 1986:348–49).

Admiration for Habermas' analytic achievements should not blind us to the fact that some of his critics have scored rather heavily. We believe that he has enriched sociology with some very useful categories and perspectives; we do not believe, however, that he has established it as a critical discipline with self-validating standards. Communicative rationality, and the possibilities for it, cannot serve as such, in view of Habermas' insistence (against Marx) that certain systemic developments should be considered as evolutionary gains. Is there any criterion which allows us to distinguish between these latter systemic developments and those which should be regarded as a nefarious 'colonisation of the Lifeworld'? Habermas' retort would probably be that the rightness of such a criterion would not be found in any of its particular characteristics but rather would be determined by the procedure by which it is established. This should be marked by communicative rationality. But could this type of formal criterion really validate a decision which might prevent its own applicability in certain areas of social life? Can a procedure in which it is established that certain systemic developments are evolutionary gains and thus should be left untouched, or even promoted, really be marked by communicative rationality? This type of rationality implies the readiness to take up debate not only with all present but also all future comers. How then could a decision on the desirability of certain systemic developments, that is, by definition, developments which will banish communicative rationality from certain areas of social life, itself be marked by this rationality? The decision excludes at least those future comers from the debate whose contribution would have been made possible by the Lifeworld circumstances now pushed out by the systemic developments deemed desirable. One can think here, in concrete terms, of such a thing as democracy in the workplace. It could be decided, for the sake of certain steering possibilities inherent in the System, to curb this democracy. Could such a decision, which whatever else it does limits certain possibilities for communicative rationality, itself be based on such rationality even though it is marked by unwillingness to accommodate certain future comers? Habermas has not made this case and we do not see how it can be made. A decision about what constitutes evolutionary gains and what does not, what is genuine emancipation and what is not, can be scientifically informed but is, in itself, not a matter of knowledge but of the will. To repeat the statement by Kolakowski we quoted above: there can be no vantage point 'from which the distinction between knowledge and will can be seen as eliminated'.

Bibliography

Abramowski, G. C. (1966) *Das Geschichtsbild Max Webers—Universalge-schichte am Leitfaden des okzidentalen Rationalisierungsprozesses* Stuttgart: Ernst Klett

Adorno Th. W. (1966) *Negative Dialektik* Frankfurt: Suhrkamp

Alford, C. F. (1985) 'Is Jürgen Habermas' Reconstructive Science Really Science' *Theory and Society* 14, 3

____ (1987) 'Habermas, Post-Freudian Psychoanalysis, and the End of the Individual' *Theory, Culture and Society* 4, 1

Bader, V. M. (1983–84) 'Schmerzlose Entkopplung von System und Lebenswelt—Engpasse der Theorie des kommunikativen Handelns von Jürgen Habermas' *Kennis en Methode* 7, 4

Baumgarten, E. (1964) *Max Weber—Werk und Person* Tübingen: J.C.B. Mohr (Paul Siebeck)

Baxter, H. (1987) 'System and Life-World in Habermas's Theory of Communicative Action' *Theory and Society* 16

Berger, J. (1982) 'Die Versprachlichung des Sakralen und die Entsprachlichung der Ökonomie' *Zeitschrift für Soziologie* 11, 4

Bernstein, R. J. (ed.) (1985) *Habermas and Modernity* Cambridge/Oxford: Blackwell

Brand, A. (1976a) *Toetsing en Kritiek—Over objectiviteit en kennisbelang bij Weber en Habermas* Meppel/Amsterdam: Boom

____ (1976b) 'Truth and Habermas' Paradigm of a Critical Social Science' *Sociologische Gids* 5

____ (1977) 'Interests and the Growth of Knowledge—A Comparison of Weber, Popper and Habermas' *Netherlands' Journal of Sociology* 13

____ (1986) 'The "Colonization of the Lifeworld" and the Disappearance of Politics: Arendt and Habermas' *Thesis Eleven* 13

____ (1987) 'Weber: Man, the Prime Mover' in D. Austin-Broos (ed.) *Creating Culture* Sydney: Allen & Unwin

____ (1987) 'Ethical Rationalisation and Juridification—Habermas' Critical Legal Theory' *The Australian Journal of Law and Society* 4

Breuer, S. (1982) 'Die Depotenzierung der kritischen Theorie—Über

Jurgen Habermas' "Theorie des kommunikativen Handelns"' *Leviathan* 10

Bubner, R. (1981) *Modern German Philosophy* Cambridge: Cambridge University Press

___ (1982a) 'Rationalität als Lebensform—Zu Jürgen Habermas' "Theorie des kommunikativen Handelns"' *Merkur* 36, 4

___ (1982b) 'Habermas's Concept of Critical Theory' in J.B. Thompson and D. Held (eds) *Habermas—Critical Debates* Basingstoke: Macmillan

Dews, P. (ed.) (1986) *Jürgen Habermas—Autonomy and Solidarity— Interviews* London: Verso

Dickens, D. R. (1983) 'The Critical Project of Jürgen Habermas' in Sabia and Wallulis (eds) *Changing Social Science. Critical Theory and Other Critical Perspectives* Albany: State University of New York Press

Eder, K. (1981) 'Zur Rationalisierungsproblematik des modernen Rechts' in W. M. Sprondel and C. Seyfarth (eds) *Max Weber und die Rationalisierung des sozialen Handelns* Stuttgart: Ernst Klett

Freitag, B. (1983) 'Theorie des kommunikativen Handelns und genetische Psychologie' *Kölner Zeitschrift für Soziologie und Sozialpsychologie* 35

Giddens, A. (1982) 'Reason Without Revolution? Habermas' *Theorie des kommunikativen Handelns*' in *Praxis International*

___ (1985) 'Reason Without Revolution? Habermas's *Theorie des kommunikativen Handelns*" in R. J. Bernstein, (ed.) *Habermas and Modernity* Cambridge/Oxford: Blackwell

Ginsberg, M. (1961) 'The Idea of Progress: a Revaluation' in *Evolution and Progress—Essays in Sociology and Social Philosophy* vol. 3, London: Heinemann

Gripp, H. (1984) *Und es gibt sie doch—Zur kommunikations-theoretischen Begründung von Vernunft bei Jürgen Habermas* München/Wien/Zurich: Paderborn

Habermas, J. (1970) 'Knowledge and Interest' in D. Emmett and A. MacIntyre (eds) *Sociological Theory and Philosophical Analysis* London

___ (1970) 'Erkenntniss und Interesse' in *Technik und Wissenschaft als Ideologie* Frankfurt a.M.: Suhrkamp

___ (1979) *Communication and the Evolution of Society* Boston: Beacon Press

___ (1981) 'Naar een reconstructie van het historisch materialisme' in *Marxisme en Filosofie* Meppel/Amsterdam: Boom

___ (1982) 'Reply to my Critics' in Thompson, J.B. and Held D. (eds) *Habermas Critical Debates* London: Basingstoke/MacMillan

___ (1984a) *The Theory of Communicative Action* vol. 1 *Reason and the Rationalization of Society* Boston: Beacon Press

___ (1984b) *Vorstudien und Ergänzungen zur Theorie des kommunikativen Handelns*, Frankfurt a.M.: Suhrkamp

___ (1985a) *Der philosophische Diskurs der Moderne—Zwölf Vorlesungen* Frankfurt a.M.: Suhrkamp

___ (1985b) 'Questions and Counterquestions' in R. J. Bernstein (ed.) *Habermas and Modernity* Cambridge/Oxford: Blackwell

_____ (1985c) 'Moral und Sittlichkeit: Hegels Kantkritik im Lichte der Diskursethik' in *Merkur* 39, 12

_____ (1986) 'Entgegnung' in A. Honneth and H. Jonas *Beiträge zu Jürgen Habermas' Theorie des kommunikativen Handelns* Frankfurt a.M.: Suhrkamp

_____ (1987) *The Theory of Communicative Action* vol. 2 *Lifeworld and System: A Critique of Functionalist Reason* Boston: Beacon Press

_____ (1988) 'Die Einheit der Vernunft in der Vielheit ihrer Stimmen' in *Merkur* 467

Haferkamp, H. (1984) 'Interaktionsaspekte, Handlungszusammenhänge und die Rolle des Wissenstransfers' in *Kölner Zeitschrift für Soziologie und Sozialpsychologie* 36

Heller, A. (1982) 'Habermas and Marxism' in J.B. Thompson and D. Held *Habermas—Critical Debates* London

Kolakowski, L. (1987) *Main Currents of Marxism* 3 vols, London: Oxford University Press

Korthals, M. and H. Kunneman (1983) 'De theorie van het communicatieve handelen: een vraaggesprek met J. Habermas' in *Kennis en Methode*

Luhmann, N. (1982) 'Autopoiesis, Handlung und kommunikative Verständigung' in *Zeitschrift für Soziologie* 11, 4

Lukács, G. (1971) *History and Class Consciousness* London: Merlin Press

Kunneman, H. (1986) *De Waarheidstrechter—Een communicatietheoretische perspectief op wetenschap en samenleving* Meppel/Amsterdam: Boom

Mayrl, W. A. (1978) 'Genetic Structuralism and the Analysis of Social Consciousness' *Theory and Society* 5

McCarthy, Th. (1985) 'Reflections on Rationalization in the Theory of Communicative Action' in R. J. Bernstein (ed.) *Habermas and Modernity* Cambridge: Polity Press

_____ (1986) 'Komplexität und Demokratie—die Versuchungen der Systemtheorie' in A. Honneth and H. Jonas *Beiträge zu Jürgen Habermas' Theorie des Kommunikativen Handelns* Frankfurt a.M.: Suhrkamp

Merton, R. K. (1957) *Social Theory and Social Structure* New York/London: The Free Press, Collier MacMillan

Parsons, T. (1967) 'The Prospects of Sociological Theory' in *Essays in Sociological Theory* New York/London: The Free Press, Collier MacMillan

Popper, K. (1972) *The Logic of Scientific Discovery* London: Hutchinson

Rocher, G. (1979) *Talcot Parsons and American Sociology* London: Thomas Nelson & Sons Ltd

Simmel, G. (1930) *Philosophie des Geldes* München/Leipzig: Duncker & Humblot

Schnädelbach, H. (1986) 'Transformation der kritischen theorie' in A. Honneth and H. Jonas (eds) *Beiträge zu Jürgen Habermas' Theorie des kommunikativen Handelns* Frankfurt a.M.: Suhrkamp

Taylor, Ch. (1986) 'Sprache und Gesellschaft' in A. Honneth and H. Jonas *Beiträge zu Jürgen Habermas' Theorie des kommunikativen Handelns* Frankfurt a.M.: Suhrkamp

Treiber, H. (1985) ' "Elective Affinities" Between Weber's Sociology of Religion and Sociology of Law' *Theory and Society* 14, 6

Weber, M. (1922) *Wirtschaft und Gesellschaft* Tübingen: J. C. B. Mohr (Paul Siebeck)

_____ (1967) *From Max Weber: Essays in Sociology* London: Routledge & Kegan Paul

_____ (1985) *Wirtschaft und Gesellschaft* Tübingen: J.C.B. Mohr

Weiss, J. (1983) 'Verständigungsorientierung und Kritik—Zur "Theorie des kommunikativen Handelns" von Jürgen Habermas' *Kölner Zeitschrift für Soziologie und Sozialpsychologie* 1

Wellmer, A. (1985) 'Reason, Utopia and the *Dialectic of Enlightenment*' in R. J. Bernstein (ed.) *Habermas and Modernity* Cambridge/Oxford: Blackwell

Whitebook, J. (1985) 'Reason and Happiness: Some Psychoanalytic Themes in Critical Theory' in R. J. Bernstein (ed.) *Habermas and Modernity* Cambridge/Oxford: Blackwell

Index